Deep Purple

UNCENSORED
ON THE RECORD

JERRY BLOOM

CODA
BOOKS LTD

C⊕DA
BOOKS LTD

www.codabooks.com

This edition is published in Great Britain in 2012 by

Coda Books Ltd., Office Suite 2, Shrieves Walk, 39 Sheep Street, Stratford-upon-Avon, Warwickshire CV37 6GJ

www.codbooks.com

Copyright © 2012 by Coda Books Ltd.

Photographs courtesy of Pictorial Press and Rex Features.

A CIP catalogue record for this book is available from the British Library.

ISBN: 978-1-78158-196-4

MUSIC ♪ REVIEWS LTD

CONTENTS

CHAPTER ONE

LISTEN, LEARN, READ ON

THE CREATION of most rock bands was either a direct result of school friendships, or through fellow musicians bumping into each other on the touring circuit. The story of the formation of Deep Purple doesn't really adhere to either of these stereotypes. Indeed, in this age of endless bands being created by record companies or marketing men, and accused of being artificially 'manufactured,' it is possible to argue that, to some extent, Deep Purple was a manufactured band. But to suggest that there is any comparison to be made with the tidal wave of 'boy' bands that emerged in the 1990s ... well, forget it. Deep Purple brought together superb musicians with enough pedigree to win Crufts!

Deep Purple's creation was the result of a brainchild of two businessmen who, having witnessed how 'popular music' had created many very wealthy individuals over the preceding decade, decided to have a crack at the music scene themselves. After all, it wasn't just individual musicians within bands such as The Beatles, The Rolling Stones and The Who who had become very wealthy, but their managers too. Among those who stood out was Colonel Tom Parker, who had masterminded the success of the first rock 'n' roll superstar, Elvis Presley. Albert Grossman had done the same with fellow American Bob Dylan, while England had its fair share of great managers, the most notable being The Beatles' Brian Epstein. By the time that John Coletta and Tony Edwards got together, Epstein had committed suicide, and fortunately, although his death shocked the rock world and shook its foundations, it didn't have fatal consequences for the genre. On the contrary, the next decade saw the rock business explode, both in financial rewards and in the excesses that many musicians indulged in. Thanks to the enterprising, if somewhat naïve, involvement of Edwards and Coletta, Deep Purple would ultimately become one of the top rock bands in the world, spearheading the second wave of world dominance by British acts.

The first wave had its roots at the beginning of the sixties, and really owed its inspiration to American rock 'n' roll pioneers such as Presley, Buddy Holly, Eddie Cochran, Chuck Berry, Jerry Lee Lewis and several others. Even though there was little media coverage when compared with today's world of saturated, twenty-four hour broadcasting, British teenagers were exposed to, and generally enraptured by, the sounds of rock 'n' roll via the odd TV show. BBC Radio's Light Programme and Radio Luxembourg were basically all that was on offer. Undoubtedly one of the most appealing aspects of the music was its rebellious image. It didn't take long for kids to find out that rock 'n' roll also annoyed the majority of their elders, and the youngsters lapped it up.

This matched the earliest musical experiences of two musicians who were living in the suburbs of West London, and who were to become founding members of Deep Purple. The first of these was Richard Hugh Blackmore. Although born in the West Country in Weston-super-Mare, Somerset on 14th April 1945, Blackmore's parents moved to Heston, Middlesex when he was just two years old. It was seeing Tommy Steele performing on 'Six-Five Special' that first got Blackmore hooked: "I wanted to play like him; I used to watch and strum along with my guitar; although I couldn't play any chords, it looked good." Blackmore had an average middle-class upbringing, and by the time that he failed his eleven-plus and missed out on attending grammar school, he was already hooked on rock 'n' roll and had cajoled his father into buying him an acoustic guitar: "I pestered my dad to get me a guitar; I'd been listening to performers like Elvis Presley on the radio, so that would have been Scotty Moore I heard playing guitar. He bought me a Framus acoustic at the local guitar shop; it cost about seven guineas, and that was a lot of money in those days."

It didn't take long for Blackmore to pick up the rudiments of the instrument, and friends of the time tell stories reflecting that, even at this early age, he was a dedicated disciple. One school friend, Valerie Morris, who still remembers Blackmore to this day, recalls: "we used to ride along to school together and he had his guitar slung over his back. He used to play it during playtime – he was very much into it. He was always playing at school, and when it was school concerts he was always up there along with everyone else." Blackmore's father insisted that his son learn the instrument properly and enrolled him for a year of classical tuition. As Morris pointed out, the young Blackmore would regularly take his guitar to school and perform with it at every opportunity. The inevitable school bands were soon formed. The first was created in the wake of the Skiffle fad, as exemplified by Lonnie Donegan, and went by the grandiose name of The Two I's Coffee Bar Junior Skiffle Group. A second Skiffle outfit called The Vampires soon followed, with Blackmore being invited to join by bassist Alan Dunklin, who lived next door but one in the Heston's street, Ash Grove. Only fourteen at the time, Blackmore was rhythm guitarist to the slightly older and more experienced Rodger Mingaye, but Mingaye soon moved on, and with his departure The Vampires changed its musical style. This was reflected in the name change to The Electric Vampires. At this time, Blackmore also badgered local guitarist Big Jim Sullivan to help him improve his talent. Sullivan was the lead guitarist with Marty Wilde and The Wildcats and was one of the most highly respected players on the scene. Blackmore would visit Sullivan's home where he learnt as much in a few hours as he had in the previous year from his classical tutor. Sullivan showed Blackmore techniques that are rarely used in classical music, such as bending the notes. He also installed into the youngster a philosophy of not copying, but allowing his own expressions to colour the music.

Within a matter of months, The Electric Vampires had changed its name again, this time to The Dominators. As an example of Blackmore's future single-minded vision, he insisted that the group should have a non-guitar-playing vocalist: rhythm player Bob Danks initially took the role on. The Dominators went through many line-up changes over its two-year existence, and at one point included a young drummer

from the area by the name of Mick Underwood. As we will see later in the story, Underwood would end up playing a pivotal role in the development of Deep Purple. Although The Dominators started while Blackmore was still at school, by the age of fifteen he had left the education system and briefly had a job at Heathrow Airport as a trainee radio mechanic. His meagre apprentice's wage was supplemented by gigs that The Dominators managed to secure within London and the Home Counties, but Blackmore had his sights set higher. In 1960 he got to see his first ever gig when he watched Nero & The Gladiators at Southall Community Centre. The Gladiators were regarded as one of the most accomplished groups of the day, and Blackmore was particularly enamoured with the band's lead guitarist, Colin Green. He even approached the band with the view of joining them, such was the impact they had upon the skinny young lad. Despite being turned down, Blackmore's determination to scale new heights remained. A few months later he applied for the role of lead guitarist in Screaming Lord Sutch & The Savages. Like The Gladiators, The Savages were equally admired as one of the top bands on the scene in 1961. The Savages were also one of the best earners, on account of their full workload: six to seven gigs, week in week out. Blackmore impressed the band's leader, David Sutch (a self-proclaimed Lord), and his band members during the audition, but he just failed to get the gig. He lost out to his former Vampires band mate Rodger Mingaye, who just had the edge, once again due to his age and extra experience.

Initially Blackmore continued with The Dominators, but in May 1961 he was offered the vacant guitarist role in Mike Dee & The Jaywalkers. Not to be confused with Peter Jay & The Jaywalkers, Mike Dee's band was not as well known, but they were nevertheless fully professional, a rarity for young bands at that time in Britain. Even at this early stage in his career,

Blackmore had built something of a reputation within the West London area, and Mike Dee was well aware of his abilities. Consequently, Blackmore had no hesitation in accepting the job and turning professional. He instantly left his job at Heathrow Airport and, with The Jaywalkers travelling around Britain in an old, beaten up Bedford van, he set out on a path that would take him to heights he could never have envisaged at the time.

Almost exactly one year later The Jaywalkers changed their name to The Condors, but, following one brief package tour, Blackmore got the gig that he really aspired to when The Savages' guitarist Bernie Watson left for a residency in Hamburg with Cliff Bennett And The Rebel Rousers. David Sutch had followed Blackmore's progress with The Jaywalkers and duly invited Blackmore to step into the role. Although it was made clear to him that it was a temporary position for six months only, it would prove to be an enormous step forward for the shy young man. Those six months taught Blackmore more about stagecraft than six years with the Jaywalkers would ever have done. Sutch was without doubt one of the most visual performers that Britain had to offer, and he insisted that his band also project a highly visual stage act. Working non-stop, gigging virtually every night of the week, Blackmore's reputation increased rapidly during this short stint.

The second musician who also grew up in the West London area, and would ultimately become a founding member of Deep Purple, was Nick Simper. Simper had seen and been impressed with Blackmore in The Jaywalkers, but recalls, "when he got into The Savages I was really pleased because The Savages was always one of my favourite bands; Ricky Brown was the best bass player around without a doubt. Carlo (Little) was definitely the top drummer; they were probably the best band on the London scene. Ritchie's individuality hadn't developed by then, he didn't have a particularly great sound or style in those days. What set Ritchie apart was pure speed; nobody could keep up with him. When he joined Sutch he started doing the fast instrumentals it was bloody great."

Simper was born a few months after Blackmore on November 3rd 1945 at Frogmore House Maternity Home in Norwood Green, Middlesex. Like Blackmore, Simper was drawn to the music scene of the day: "I guess it all started with Lonnie Donegan. Like most young people in the 1950's, I was completely knocked out by the excitement of his records. My first record purchase was Lonnie's 'Gambling Man', on 78 rpm of course, which survived for two days until it was dropped and smashed in two!" While on a family holiday in Devon in

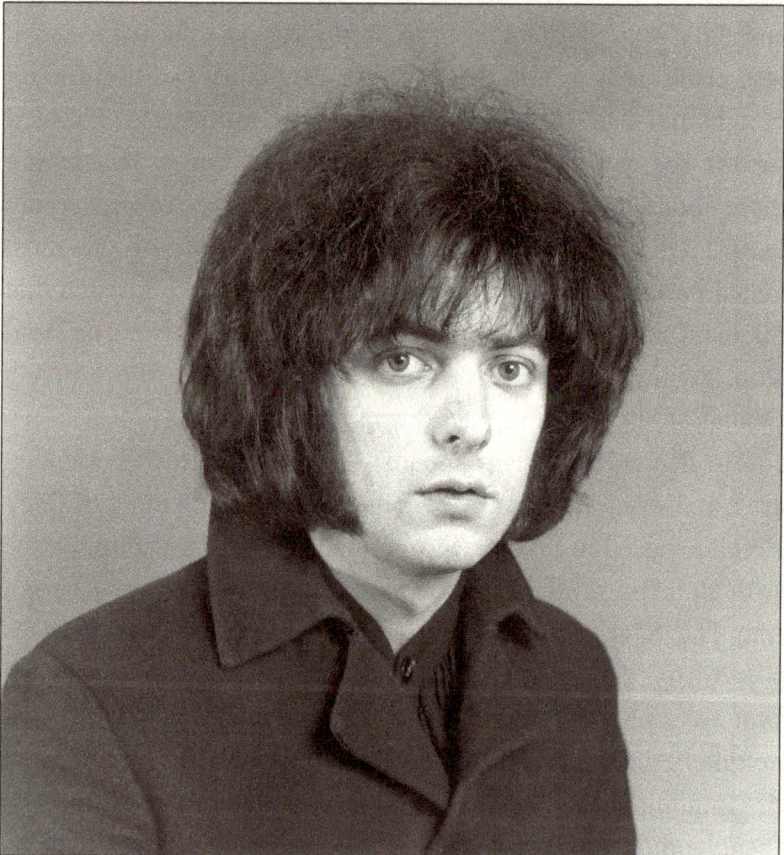

1959, Simper was first exposed to the sound that would have a profound effect on his future musical direction: "An amazing disc called 'Please Don't Touch' by Johnny Kidd & The Pirates, which I could not get enough of. Little did I know back then as a twelve year old, that one day I would be a member of the Pirates!"

The similarities with Blackmore's musical development were uncanny. While on holiday with his family, Simper's father, fully aware of his son's passion for music, promised to buy him a guitar. Like Blackmore, it would also be a Framus and, having invested a small fortune of 17 guineas on the instrument, Simper's father insisted that he learnt to play it properly: "Dad enrolled me for lessons with a middle-aged gent called Bert Kirby. Bert taught me to read music, but I soon discovered that it was quicker to pick up the hit tunes by ear, so I dispensed with Bert, much to Dad's relief, as the lessons weren't cheap!"

Like so many young musicians, Simper aspired to be the next Duane Eddy or Hank Marvin and, by 1960, while still at school, he joined his first band called The Renegades, playing lead guitar. The Renegades included Adam Faith's cousin Ian Nelhams on drums. However, the band soon disintegrated as regular band members were hard to retain and gigs dried up. Simper then joined a semi-pro outfit called The Delta Five, and it was during this time that he first came into contact with Blackmore, catching him at the Southall Community Centre with The Jaywalkers. It was around this time that Simper also came into contact with a man who would help to shape British rock as much as anyone. "Bert Kirby, my old tutor, had introduced me to a friend of his who was about to open a music shop in Hanwell, West London. His friend was a drum teacher called Jim Marshall. His little shop at 76, Uxbridge Road soon became a Mecca for budding musicians and top professionals alike." It was at Jim Marshall's store that Simper acquired his first electric guitar: "I had agreed to buy John MacDonald's Futurama (lead guitarist with The Travellers), which Jim Marshall had promised me at the trade-in price of 20 guineas. Of course finding 20 guineas was out of the question, but Jim kindly let me take the guitar away on the agreement that I would pay £1 per week, precisely the amount that I received from my Saturday job in the local butcher's shop! Every weekend I would cycle to Jim's shop and give him a one-pound note. He would duly fill in the card, until one day, after half the payments had been made, he wrote in large letters - PAID! across the card, and the Futurama was mine! This became a pattern of generosity, which Jim showed throughout the early years of his business, and so it is no surprise that his customers stayed loyal, and later flocked to buy his amplifiers, making Marshall one of the most recognised names in the business.

Simper got the opportunity to turn professional in late '64 when he joined Buddy Britten And The Regents, switching to bass guitar in the process and recording two singles with the band, released on the Piccadilly label in 1965. Within less than a year Britten changed the band's name to the Simon Raven Cult, recording one more single, but Simper was to get his first really big break in May 1966 when he joined Johnny Kidd and the (New) Pirates, as they were to be billed. For Simper it was a dream come true, performing alongside one of his idols and one of Britain's finest rock 'n' roll performers. Kidd was arguably responsible for producing the finest British rock 'n' roll record of the era, the classic 1960 hit 'Shakin' All Over.'

Meanwhile, Blackmore's career had seen him move on from The Savages to The Outlaws, one of Britain's most well-known bands, famous for backing the likes of John Leyton on hit records such as 'Johnny Remember Me.' The Outlaws were the resident session band for eccentric, genius, independent producer Joe Meek. Blackmore and a former band mate, drummer Mick

Underwood, joined the band in October '62, teaming up with the existing Outlaws, rhythm guitarist Ken Lundgren and bassist Chas Hodges. Blackmore stayed with the band until early '64, developing his skills doing hundreds of sessions for the hordes of artists that came and went from Meek's makeshift studio, situated above a leather shop in London's Holloway Road. Freddie Starr and Tom Jones were just two of the famous artists for whom Blackmore backed. The Outlaws also produced their own singles, as well as backing legendary US rockers Jerry Lee Lewis and Gene Vincent during their British concert tours. The combination of the discipline developed in studio situations with the stage performances with the great American icons would hold Blackmore in great stead as the years progressed.

One of Meek's most well known artists was Heinz Burt, the former bass player with The Tornados, who enjoyed a relatively successful solo career. Heinz's career peaked in August '63 with the top ten hit 'Just Like Eddie' that featured backing by The Outlaws, with Blackmore's inimitable guitar work to the fore. Blackmore left the Outlaws in early '64 to join a full-time backing band for Heinz called the Wild Ones, although the name was soon changed to the Wild Boys after it was established that there was an American band with the same name. Blackmore's career then went through a period of uncertainty over the next couple of years. Firstly he became dissatisfied backing Heinz, who was not in truth a particularly talented artist. Studio work would come and go, but live gigs with a host of bands helped to keep the wolf from the door. Initially he took a gig as part of Neil Christian's band The Crusaders, before jumping ship with fellow band members Arvid Andersen and Jimmy Evans, and briefly returning in Sutch's latest incarnation of The Savages. Following a residency in Germany backing Jerry Lee Lewis, Blackmore went back and forth between The Crusaders and The Savages, with the exception of one three-month Italian jaunt backing local artist Riki Maiocchi under the name of The Trips. Much of Blackmore's live work between '65 and '67 was in Germany, where he eventually set up home for about a year, living at his girlfriend's flat in Hamburg.

For Nick Simper, his glorious gig with Johnny Kidd came to a quick and abrupt end on 7th October 1966. That evening the band was booked for a gig in Bolton, but they arrived late, just as the doors were opening. Despite there being only a few people around and sufficient time to set up, the manager saw this as a serious breach of contract. Despite Kidd's offer to waive his personal fee and arrange for just the band to be paid, the manager cancelled the show outright. As a result, they trooped to the nearby Nelson Imperial where they always had a good rapport with the manager. Just after midnight, while travelling back from their hastily arranged gig, the car carrying Kidd and Simper was involved in a collision three miles south of Bury, Lancashire. Traffic was diverted while firemen cut the injured from the wreckage and rushed them to hospital. Simper was hospitalised with lacerations, head and back injuries, plus a badly smashed-up arm, but Johnny Kidd, whose real name was Frederick Heath, was tragically pronounced dead on arrival. After making a full recovery, Simper and his fellow band mates continued to promote Kidd's legacy as The Pirates, but this only lasted for a few months as the music scene was rapidly changing. The old school rock 'n' roll was losing favour to a new breed, spearheaded by the likes of Cream and Jimi Hendrix, with an emphasis on power, virtuosity and lengthy, complex musical jams.

Such musical styles would have been alien to Jon Douglas Lord as he grew up in Leicester during and immediately after the Second World War. Lord was born on the 9th of June 1941 and, coming from a musical family, by 1948 his parents had enrolled him for piano lessons. Unlike many kids, who soon tire of the rigid structures of formal tuition, Lord stuck with the lessons for ten years, attaining all the grades in the process and passing the Royal Academy of Music exams, as well as getting an 'A' level in music at Grammar school. But Lord's love of music accompanied an interest in another of the arts, and he had serious ambitions to become an actor. Upon leaving school, he took a job as a clerk in a solicitor's office, and he spent some of the money earned on records. His musical tuition had developed a healthy love for classical music but, on hearing Jerry Lee Lewis, his mind was opened up to the world of rock 'n' roll. Several years later he commented, "the first four bars of 'Whole Lotta Shakin' Going On' totally turned my head around.

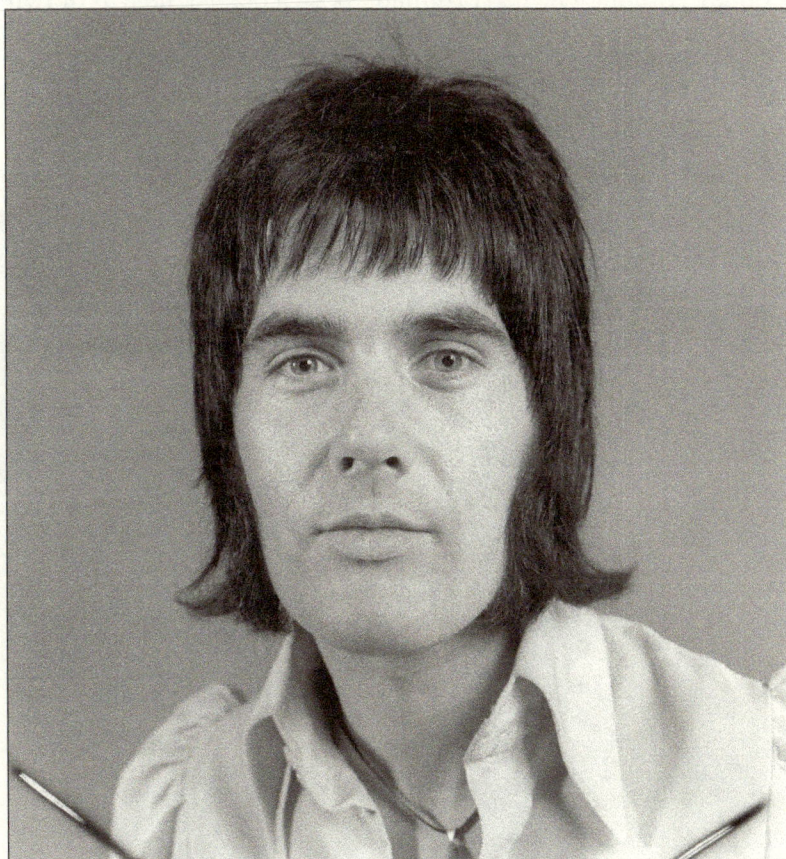

I tried like hell to make the old piano at home sound like that but it wouldn't. That's when I realised there was more to rock 'n' roll than meets the ear."

After some time, Lord was fired from his day job for taking too much time off and, despite his new found love for rock 'n' roll, he applied for and was accepted as a student at the Central School of Speech And Drama in Swiss Cottage, London. A couple of years later, Lord moved on to the newly formed London Drama Centre, and during this time he also put his musical talent to use playing in pubs in a jazz group called the Bill Ashton Combo. Lord soon gravitated towards an r 'n' b act called Red Bludd's Bluesicians, also known as The Don Wilson Combo. Although he had originally been a pianist, he was drawn

to the organ after hearing legendary jazz player Jimmy Smith. "That's what turned me on to the organ. I heard 'Walk On The Wild Side' and I didn't know what that instrument was. I found out it was a Hammond and I found out I couldn't afford one, so I managed to buy an organ of sorts. With a little beefing up it was made to sound roughly like a Hammond," he explained to Circus magazine in 1974.

After his initial stint with The Don Wilson Combo, the band teamed up with leader of The Art Wood Combo, the elder brother of future Faces and Rolling Stones guitarist Ronnie Wood. They adopted the name The Artwoods and went professional in the autumn of 1964. Following a record deal with Decca the band appeared on 'Ready Steady Go,' and eventually cut seven singles, an EP and one LP. Although they proved to be a popular live act, The Artwoods only achieved moderate success. Like all jobbing musicians of the day, Lord also took whatever session work came his way, and producer Shel Talmy drafted him in to provide piano on The Kinks' 'You Really Got Me.' "All I did was plink, plink, plink. It wasn't hard," joked Lord when talking about it thirty-six years later. As with sessions in general, he was paid a one-off fee. This proved disappointing for the young, financially struggling musician because the song became a number one hit in the summer of 1964! Coincidentally, thanks to the powerful guitar riff, some also credit the song as being the prototype for the heavy rock style that Deep Purple would become one of the greatest exponents of.

The other two musicians who would become part of the first Deep Purple line-up were based a few miles west of England's capital city, which was the centre of the music business. Rod Evans was born in Edinburgh on 19th January 1947, but when Rod was still a nipper, the family moved south to Slough in Berkshire. Vocalist Evans took his cues from Cliff Bennett and The Hollies' Allan Clarke. His first band, The Horizons, were sufficiently good enough to play the clubs in Hamburg. After their drummer quit, the band had no hesitation in approaching a young drummer from a small-time band, The Shindigs. Ian Anderson Paice was born in Nottingham on the 29th of June 1948. Paice's father worked for the civil service and, after a three-year contract in Germany, the family returned to England to set up home in Bicester, Oxfordshire when Ian was just seven years old. Like Jon Lord, Paice grew up in a musical family and his father had played piano in dance bands during the thirties and forties. From an early age he had a natural desire to hit things and, once the furniture had suffered more abuse than his parents could accept, Ian's father invested a small fortune in his first drum kit. It turned out to be more than a passing fad and, by the time he was fifteen, Paice would sometimes play with his father's band on a Saturday night, earning a few bob in the process. Growing up with this style of music helped to develop a natural swing to his playing, a style that has been influential throughout his career and one that few rock drummers employ.

Ian Paice's first rock 'n' roll band was Georgie and The Rave Ons, who gigged around the Oxford area and changed its name to The Shindigs by 1965. Although The Shindigs released a couple of singles, when they supported Rod Evans's band on several occasions, Paice became aware how much more professional Evans's band were and jumped at the opportunity to join. It was a wise decision as, soon after, not only did The Horizons change its name to MI5, but it also got a deal with Parlophone Records and cut its first single, 'You'll Never Stop Me Loving You.' Another name change to The Maze appeared to help the band progress further, and trips to Germany and Italy ensued.

It was during one of these trips that Ian Paice first bumped into Ritchie Blackmore on board the ferry to Hamburg. The Maze was on its way to Italy and, after working there for three months, got a three-week stint at Hamburg's famous Star Club, where once again Blackmore and Paice crossed paths. This time Blackmore got to see the drummer perform live and was duly impressed with his flashy style. Blackmore was pretty restless at this stage in his life: very little work was coming his way, and he spent most of his time just practising and jamming with bands at the Star Club. Having spent the past six years as a backing musician, he was desperate to get his own band together and offered Paice the role of drummer. Paice declined as, in truth, Blackmore had no band, and The Maze was earning sufficiently good money that Paice wasn't prepared to leave it for a speculative project. In 1972 Paice spoke to Disc magazine saying, "This is where I ran into Ritchie Blackmore. He'd been there a year, sort of stagnating. He sent his girlfriend up to me and she said Ritchie would like to offer me a job – Ritchie does things like this. I went, 'Oh really!' 'cos I'd heard of him, Ritchie Blackmore. I thought great, so I said, 'what's he got?' She said he didn't have a band yet, so I said I was sorry and went back home."

It was now 1967, and back in England both Jon Lord and Nick Simper wound up in the same band: 'The Garden' was the backing band for The Flowerpot Men, who were cashing in on their 'flower power' hit single, 'Let's Go To San Francisco.' Following Kidd's death and the subsequent failure of The Pirates to continue without their influential leader, Simper initially teamed up with The Savages' drummer Carlo Little backing Billie Davies. They toured in Germany where, like Paice, Simper also bumped into Blackmore: "When I was working with Billie Davis we had Ged Peck with us who was no slouch, but Carlo was always pushing Ritchie to me. We bumped into Ritchie and he was doing nothing at all. Carlo said, 'Why don't Nick and me come over. We'll live in Hamburg a bit?' Because he was getting a reputation, just by walking up to the Star Club and sitting in with people and jamming. He could get up and blow everybody away and just walk away like the man in black, like a gunfighter. Carlo talked him into that but the only reason we didn't go was because to get it going I was going to handle the vocals, keep it a three-piece but at the time I got afflicted with this terrible tonsillitis. Even with Billie Davis I was just singing backing harmonies but I would get a sore throat and I couldn't speak for a week so there was no way I could have gone out and do ten or fifteen numbers singing so we abandoned it."

Meanwhile Jon Lord's group, The Artwoods, had taken the decision to cash in on the gangster fad following the success of the 'Bonnie And Clyde' film, and renamed themselves The St Valentine's Day Massacre. It proved to be a total flop in the UK, although Denmark welcomed the new act with open arms. A number one single over there ensured a lengthy Scandinavian tour, but the band couldn't sustain its newfound success and soon folded. Lord took what little session work was available. He worked with producer Gus Dudgeon (who later went on to produce Elton John), co-writing three songs that found their way onto a 'Blues Anthology' album that also included Cyril Davis, Jeff Beck, Jimmy Page and Eric Clapton. The three tracks were performed by Santa Barbera Machine Head, a band that saw Lord teaming up with guitarist Ronnie Wood, Kim Gardener (bass) and 'Twink' (John Alder) from The Pretty Things on drums. On the album's sleeve notes, Dudgeon claimed that the band was born five years earlier and "died after a bad attack of talent." It's fair to say that some degree of poetic licence was used to hype up the recordings. Lord also did a session for Decca producer Mike Vernon, who had produced The Artwoods. Lord provided organ on an album of instrumental interpretations of pop and Motown classics of the day. Billed as being by The Leading Figures, the now incredibly rare album 'Sound And Movement' was produced with the sole purpose of being a party record, and was a precursor to the K-Tel 'Non-Stop Party Hits' that proliferated through the early seventies. Times were hard and sessions such as these helped to earn a few bob but, fortunately for Lord, a more lucrative gig as part of The Garden arose when the group's keyboard player Billy Davidson was hospitalised. Lord willingly took the role of organist, teaming up with Nick Simper in the process.

1967 would prove to be a pivotal year for rock music. In February, Blackmore's former employer, producer Joe Meek, went out in a blaze of publicity, shooting his landlady before turning the shotgun on himself. Although Meek had several problems that contributed in pushing him over the edge, his brand of pop was losing favour and, like many who had helped to shape the first half of the decade's musical landscape, he

wasn't moving with the times. The black American guitarist Jimi Hendrix was one of the key new artists taking the music world by storm. Although his first hit, 'Hey Joe,' entered the UK charts in the last week of December '66, it was 1967 that would prove to be the year when Hendrix burst onto the scene and captured the public's imagination with his uninhibited approach. The music scene was changing rapidly; many musicians saw a life outside the three-minute pop tunes. An emphasis on virtuosity and more complex compositions were pushing the boundaries of what could be achieved. The Beatles were as quick as anyone to move with the times, and in the summer of '67 released the groundbreaking 'Sgt Pepper's Lonely Hearts Club Band.'

Blackmore observed that, with the changing face of popular music, the opportunity to showcase his undoubted talent, developed from years on the road, was just around the corner. Harmony bands such as The Hollies and The Searchers were no longer hogging the limelight and, with the focus now firmly on musicianship, Blackmore was confident he could achieve the same level of success that Hendrix and Cream's Eric Clapton were attaining. While in Hamburg, he made his first attempts to put a band together. Spending so much time at the Star Club, Blackmore was able to pick musicians he thought would be ideal for the type of band he had in mind.

He drafted in a German bass player by the name of Kurt Lungen and, on drums, a Scotsman named Ricky Munro who was doing a month's residency with his band The Rite Tyme. Munro recalls the type of music they were working on: "He spoke a lot about American black blues, he loved that. The numbers we were doing ourselves, the original ones were mainly based on things he had gleaned off these old black blues players. I was pretty sure he was very much influenced by that, a more modern equivalent. One number had to have a drum solo in it. A lot of it was just jamming and he also had ideas for songs. We just followed our noses and the ones that turned out to be quite exciting became a permanent fixture in the set list." One number they worked on called 'Mandrake Root' was to be the name of the band, but sadly the project never got beyond a few rehearsals and Mandrake Root never performed live.

It is no coincidence that harmony bands such as The Searchers have been mentioned because, ironically, it was due to the involvement of The Searchers' ex-drummer-cum-vocalist Chris Curtis that the Deep Purple machine initially came into being. While Blackmore was in Germany, frustrated that his musical ideas were not coming to fruition, back in England Curtis had grand ideas. Like Blackmore, Chris Curtis had worked the Hamburg scene, but by 1966 he had quit The Searchers and had other musical visions. Somewhat fortuitously, Curtis moved into a flat in Gunter Grove, Fulham, South West London. The large building was home to several musicians including Denny Laine from The Moody Blues, as well as Jon Lord. Curtis talked to Lord about his vision for a band based on the concept of a roundabout, with a revolving turnaround of musicians. The most important thing that Curtis did was to introduce Lord to his financial backer, Tony Edwards. Curtis had already sold the idea to Edwards, who at the time ran a family textile business. Edwards had already dabbled in the pop business, taking on the roll of manager for up and coming singer Ayshea Hague. Hague's singing career never took off, although she did host the long-running ITV show 'Lift Off.' More importantly, Edwards's involvement in trying to promote her career had brought him into contact with Chris Curtis. No doubt Edwards saw that it was worth taking a risk, as Curtis was already an established name in the business. Furthermore, Curtis brushed shoulders with many of the big names, including The Beatles, and Edwards duly agreed to invest in Curtis's musical roundabout idea.

Although convinced of the potential, Edwards was also aware how much cash would be needed and, seeing that it may be too much for one man financially, he brought in his friend John Coletta as a fellow investor. Coletta was the managing director of Castle, Chappel & Partners, an advertising and marketing consultancy. As well as agreeing to involve himself, Coletta also suggested a third investor and brought in a used car salesman, Ron Hire. The initials of their surnames created the company that was to be known as HEC Enterprises.

Although Curtis had some undoubtedly wacky ideas, most probably the results of mind-altering substances, he did have at least one sensible plan, namely to involve a superb guitarist who was languishing in the seedy St Pauli district of Hamburg. Curtis had crossed paths with Blackmore a few years earlier when The Searchers performed at the Star Club, and even though Blackmore's name was relatively unknown in his homeland, the musicians' circle was more than familiar with his talents. Even Eric Clapton had crossed paths with Blackmore in late '66. During one of his stints with Screaming Lord Sutch, the Blackmore-led Savages had wound up as the support act for Cream at Sussex University in Brighton. As The Savages' bass player Tony Dangerfield recalled: "We shared what was a classroom as a dressing room and we pulled all the stops out that night. I'll never forget this: Ritchie walked into the dressing room and Clapton's picking his Les Paul up and Ritchie heard him say, 'fuck it I don't know why I'm bothering going on.' Ritchie had pulled all the stops out and we got thrown off that tour. They had us off straight away. Ritchie knew that he was better and he proved it. Put his money where his mouth was that night."

The incredible levels of self-belief and, to some degree, arrogance that were displayed would prove invaluable over the next few years and ensure that Deep Purple made it to the very top. This self-belief also meant that, when Blackmore received an invitation to come to England and check out the new band being put together by Chris Curtis, he wasn't initially convinced with what he saw. On the plus side, it did bring Blackmore into contact with Jon Lord and the pair immediately struck up a good working relationship. However, Curtis's ideas and behaviour were becoming more irrational by the day. His idea for a musical roundabout with other musicians coming and going as they please certainly caused some concerns for Jon Lord. Lord saw that it could be a very short-term experience. Several years ago, he explained the way Curtis described that it would work: "It would just be the three of us as the core, and the reason it would be called Roundabout was that other musicians would jump on

and jump off as we chose to have them in the band, and he sold the idea to Tony Edwards." Lord was worried that he might well be one of those who soon found himself off the roundabout, although Curtis said, "no Jon you and me will be the core of the roundabout." It may have seemed like a somewhat fanciful idea, but, as Lord explained in 1995, "please do remember this was 1967!" It certainly was, at the height of the flower power explosion, free love and all that, and such thinking was not uncommon. But before long, Curtis drifted out of the equation. Tony Edwards remained sufficiently enthralled by the prospect of managing a rock band that he agreed to continue to give Jon Lord his support in recruiting the required musicians. Realising that there was sufficient financial investment in the project, Blackmore was also keen to keep things afloat as he saw that the opportunity at last to do just what he wanted was potentially about to see the light of day.

- CHAPTER TWO -
THE STARS BEGIN
TO FLICKER

ALTHOUGH BLACKMORE could see his days of financial struggle potentially coming to an end, he wasn't about to jump into the situation until the musicians who would be involved were fully established. One night at London's Speakeasy club he bumped into well-respected drummer Bobby Woodman, whose career went back to the late fifties and the 2 I's Coffee Bar scene. As Woodman recalled, "he gave me the details of this band he was forming and asked me if I was interested in joining. I asked what sort of band are you in? Because I'm a rockabilly drummer. He said, 'We're a rock 'n' roll band, funded by millionaire businessmen.'" Woodman in turn approached bassist / vocalist Dave Curtiss and invited him to check the situation out. Curtiss remembers, "I met Jon Lord and Ritchie Blackmore sitting on a bed, going through ideas for about a week or ten days. Bobbie and I were a good unit, and I would have been a really good bass player for them, but Jon asked if I was as good as some big star like Jack Bruce. I said I didn't compare myself to anyone, which was obviously not what he wanted to hear!"

Through Lord's involvement with The Flowerpot Men, Blackmore also decided to check out one of their gigs to see if Lord was as good live as he had been during their initial meeting at Lord's flat in London. He also had the opportunity to check out Lord's band mate Nick Simper, who was potentially in the frame as well. Lord had put the proposition to Simper after a gig in Holland, and when he explained that the band would involve both Blackmore and Woodman, Simper jumped at the opportunity.

HEC Enterprises put their money where their mouth was and invested heavily in providing the new band with the necessary equipment: a Hammond organ for Jon Lord, and as much amplification as was required to ensure that, when the band were ready to go on stage, audiences were definitely going to hear what they had to offer. HEC also rented Deeves Hall, an old farmhouse in South Mimms, Hertfordshire where the band could live and rehearse. Co-manager John Coletta recalled in the early seventies how it all kicked off: "We put them into a farmhouse and got the equipment together and they got the act together. We bought everything from Marshall's. There was about £7,000 in total with the Hammond organ and everything. We rented the farmhouse for about six weeks, which cost us something like £50 a week without food. Tony had dabbled in pop with a girl singer called Ayshea and launched her first record, so he had a little bit of knowledge about the business. We were very green, I personally had no involvement at all except when I was a student I used to play in a group."

There was also the small matter of finding a vocalist, which would prove to be a lengthy process.

Although the exact details seem to be buried in nearly forty years of history, solo vocalist Terry Reid was the first to be approached. Reid has gone down in rock history for not only turning down what would become Deep Purple, but a year later he also rejected Jimmy Page's invitation to join Led Zeppelin, and in doing so suggested Robert Plant in the process. The guys had put out feelers to Reid's manager but were told that he was not interested. It is generally considered that manager Mickie Most had such a tight control over Reid, that even if he wanted the job, Most was determined to retain him as a solo performer. Reid himself cannot recall the series of events very clearly, and is even unsure whether or not he was in the frame when Deep Purple first started off or the following year when the band underwent its first line-up change, but Nick Simper clearly remembers he was the first vocalist they approached. When speaking to Classic Rock magazine in 2006 Reid said: "I'm not sure what frame I was in when I was asked. I think it was when Ritchie was doing it at the beginning, or maybe afterwards, or maybe in between. I had gone to California and it's all a bit vague. But Blackmore was a brilliant guitar player. I saw him in Screaming Lord Sutch's Savages. Sutch used to chase him around the stage with an axe. Ritchie never used to miss a note and that ain't an easy thing to do. Not when you are about to be beheaded! Blackmore had a terrible job being a member of that band."

Nick Simper then suggested a vocalist from the same West London area that both he and Blackmore came from. Ian Gillan was someone that Simper had seen many years earlier when the young singer was performing under the name of Jess Thunder with his band The Javelins. By 1968 he had reverted to using

his real name as lead singer with the pop outfit Episode Six. The group had recorded several singles, and had also appeared on the German TV show 'The Beat Club.' When Gillan was approached and invited to audition for the newly created band he declined, believing that Episode Six, as an already established band was going to hit the big time, and had little reason to believe this new group would achieve much success.

Several other names were bandied about including one Rod Stewart. Stewart at the time was singing in the Jeff Beck Group and the guys went to check him out at London's Marquee club on 20th February. Blackmore was, and indeed still is to this day, a great admirer of Beck's guitar skills, but none of the band was suitably impressed with Stewart to even offer him an audition! It's probably worth mentioning that Stewart had also been one of the many vocalists to enter Joe Meek's studios several years earlier but the maverick producer was also unimpressed with the self-proclaimed 'Scottish' singer!

When they resorted to placing adverts in Melody Maker, hordes of singers applied for the job. Nick Simper had the task of collecting them from Borehamwood Railway station and ferrying the potentials to the remote farmhouse a few miles away. Amongst the many who applied was Mick Angus, who sang with a Slough based band. Angus was close to getting the job, indeed so confident that he had actually got it that he told his close friends in fellow Slough band The Maze, including singer Rod Evans. Evans then took the opportunity to apply for the gig himself and, to the surprise of Angus, was offered the job. Evans impressed the majority of the band not just with his vocal abilities, but also with his song writing ideas, in particular his idea to do The Beatles 'Help' as a ballad. However, Woodman wasn't so impressed by The Maze's front man: "Rod Evans got up and sang some Frank Sinatra numbers and I thought, 'we don't want this kind of singer.'"

Although Evans's appointment as lead singer completed the five-man outfit, the rest of the band were becoming increasingly disillusioned with Bobby Woodman. Blackmore, Lord and Simper were drawn to the sounds of Hendrix, and in particular the American East Coast band Vanilla Fudge, with its leanings towards psychedelia and lengthy instrumental jams. Woodman, who had worked with traditional rock 'n' roll stars like Vince Taylor and Johnny Hallyday, was at odds with the musical direction the band was heading in. In recent years, Woodman has openly admitted that he wasn't happy with the way things were developing: "They played this song and I said, 'You sound like a fucking circus band! Can we play something that's to do with the band and stop wasting time?'" Fortunately the arrival of Rod Evans gave the guys the opportunity to try out another drummer. As Lord recalled, "Rod pulled me to one side and said, 'Our drummer Ian is a much better drummer than Bobby.'" Blackmore also remembered seeing The Maze in Hamburg the previous year, and so Ian Paice was brought along to try out for the group. In 1972, Paice recalled the series of events from his perspective: "Rod said he had an audition with this new band and he was leaving." The Maze was earning good money for the time, going out for £5 a night, and they weren't keen to jack it in. "Rod took me to one side and said, 'look they've got a drummer at the moment but I think they'll like you better.' So I went along and found out that it was Blackmore."

In the first of what would be many underhand shenanigans, Ian Paice was auditioned behind Woodman's back. One night Jon Lord enticed teetotaller Woodman to go to the pub with him: "he said, 'I fancy a drink and I don't want to go by myself,' and he practically forced me. I noticed a new drum kit by the front door as we were leaving, and asked myself, 'what are they doing there?' About an hour later we came back, and I saw the whole band playing with a new drummer, Ian Paice." Paice instantly impressed the guys and seemed far more in tune with what they were working towards. "I knew it was something good happening and I wanted it," Paice said simply years later. It was left to the inexperienced management team to notify Woodman that his services were no longer required: "The managers called me in for a meeting. They told me they didn't need my style of drumming, "so any time you like, please get your things and move out." Woodman was livid, as he had just given up his flat to move into Deeves Hall, and was down on his luck financially. "They offered me twenty quid. I said, 'You must be fucking joking!' So they made it forty quid."

With a new drummer in the shape of the young but receptive Ian Paice, a stable line-up was now complete, and they continued rehearsing a live set and writing new songs. The only other thing left to do was to find a suitable name. Tony Edwards still supported Chris Curtis's idea of Roundabout, but the others were less impressed. Over the ensuing weeks several ideas were suggested, and all were duly written down on a piece of paper. Some of them certainly reflected the psychedelic ambience of the times; Orpheus and Concrete God were two that Jon Lord recalled many years later. Another strong candidate for a while was Fire, no doubt inspired by the Hendrix song of the same name that appeared on his debut album 'Are You Experienced,' released in May '67. One name that Ritchie Blackmore favoured was 'Deep Purple,' the title of a well-known song originally composed in 1933 by pianist Peter De Rose. It had served many artists well, including Bing Crosby in 1939. It had also been a moderate hit in 1957 for Billy Ward and his Dominoes, but Nino Tempo and April Stevens arguably had the biggest success with the song in 1963. 'Deep Purple' was a favourite of Ritchie Blackmore's grandmother, and in the words of Jon Lord, she would say to her grandson, "This new band you've got, are you going to play my favourite song, 'Deep Purple'?"

Of course, the song wasn't remotely suited for the style of music the band was leaning towards, but as a name for the group it might just do. Names aside, the most important thing was to create a set of material that would slay the audiences. Simper and Blackmore in particular were also very concerned about having a visual impact. Through his stints with Screaming Lord Sutch's Savages, Blackmore had learnt all about stage movements and how to work a crowd over. Now he was in a band with top quality musicians, the combination of visuals with top quality musicianship couldn't possibly fail. In the two months spent at Deeves Hall a mixture of new songs and re-workings of several covers were worked out. Blackmore resurrected the 'Mandrake Root' song he had come up with the year before, although it wasn't entirely original. "Mandrake Root was written by a guy called Bill Parkinson and it was called 'Lost Soul' originally," explains Nick Simper. "He was with Sutch before Ritchie and they used to do that as one of the opening numbers. When Ritchie took over, Carlo taught him the melody note for note, sung it to him. Ritchie said, 'what about this?' I said, 'that's Bill's number Lost Soul.' 'Not now it isn't.' I said 'you won't get away with that' but the attitude was 'just watch me.'"

Just a matter of days after recruiting Ian Paice, the band went into Trident Studios to record two demo tracks for presentation to potential labels. Recorded in one take each, the two tracks didn't actually get commercially released until they appeared on a compilation album in 1985. Considering the short time they had to work on the arrangements, both 'Shadows' and 'Love Help Me' were sufficiently powerful enough recordings to stoke up record company interest, despite the fact that the vocals on the latter were mistakenly omitted when the engineer mixed the track for the acetate, turning it into an instrumental in the process. Even before the demo had been made, Jon Lord had approached his old Artwoods producer, Mike Vernon at Decca, who had agreed to sign them just on the strength of hearing the four of them rehearse while Woodman was still in the line-up.

None of the management team of HEC Enterprises had sufficient knowledge of the business to set the ball rolling, so Blackmore contacted an old friend, Derek Lawrence, by then an established producer working for EMI. Blackmore had originally crossed paths with Lawrence during his session days for Joe Meek. Lawrence worked alongside Meek for a while before branching out on his own, and had also roped Blackmore in on many sessions for his own productions, so the pair were very familiar with each other's work. At Blackmore's invitation,

Derek Lawrence visited the lads at Deeves Hall and set about establishing recording contracts. Through his array of invaluable connections, Lawrence took the Trident Studios demo recording to Roy Featherstone at EMI and a deal was secured, with the band signed to EMI's Parlophone label. In doing this, they became instant stable mates with The Beatles. Through Lawrence a deal was also secured for the American market, but in this case he didn't need to hawk the demo around as a newly formed label approached him, requesting he found them a new British band. Tetragrammaton was largely created from the finances of comedian Bill Cosby, and it was Lawrence's associate Artie Mogul, a man who was involved in Bob Dylan's UK publishing, who had been given the job of securing new acts.

Thirty years later, Jon Lord reflected on these formative days in the band to Keyboard magazine: "Chris Curtis decided that he wanted to stop being a Merseybeat musician. He wanted to be part of the 'London scene.' At the time, I was playing in the backing band for the Flowerpot Men, as some sort of penance for all my earlier sins. Chris introduced me to Ritchie Blackmore and a rich businessman who wanted to invest in a pop band, and then he suddenly went a little bonkers and disappeared. So Chris was the catalyst – he wandered into my life, changed it, and wandered out again. Meeting Ritchie was obviously the turning point in my life, and by the spring of '68 we had a band together."

With a live set now worked out (through the popularity of The Artwoods in Denmark), Jon Lord's contacts enabled them to set up a debut tour of Scandinavia. Much capital was made from the new band being promoted as ex-Artwoods, although they still didn't actually have a name. Roundabout kept getting used, largely pushed forward by HEC, but the band was still unhappy with it. Although the name wouldn't have meant much to Danish audiences, a children's TV show called

'The Magic Roundabout' had been popular in Britain since it was first aired in October '65, and it's quite feasible that the band was concerned that Roundabout might give the wrong impression! Lord's recollection was that they planned to go to Denmark as Roundabout, and if the tour was a disaster, they could come back and change the name. However, on the ferry over, Simper and Blackmore in particular were disillusioned that they were constantly being referred to as Roundabout, and the name Deep Purple that Blackmore had written down while at Deeves Hall was re-activated. Blackmore got his way, not for the last time, and it was agreed by all that when they got to Denmark they would push forward Deep Purple and renounce the name Roundabout.

Irrespective of the name, the fact that the tour was promoted as ex-Artwoods was the most important factor in ensuring the new band would play to reasonable sized crowds from the off. However, even before they got to play the first gig, as the ferry docked in Esbjerg, their arrival in Denmark was a rather inauspicious event. As Ian Paice recalled, "you needed a work permit and ours wasn't quite in order." Their roadie Ian Hansford still has a smirk on his face to this day as he vividly remembers, "they all had to get in the back of a police van." Ian Paice remembered: "We were taken from the docks to the police station in the back of a police-dog van, behind the wire grill." Fortunately the problems with the permits were soon sorted out and they were ready to play their first gig. The promoters had done their job and the first gig in a school hall in Tastrup on 20th April was packed. Several local papers were there to cover the event and the amount of equipment they had squeezed onto the tiny stage prompted one reviewer to describe it as looking like "something out of a science fiction story." Much was made of the band's volume, and when Jon Lord was interviewed by a Danish journalist he explained, "I know we're loud on stage but you need to reach the youth of today. We're not just loud for the sake of being loud, you just have to make sure the people don't think they're at a tea party, because then they'll lose interest."

With the collective experience of the musicians involved, there wasn't much likelihood that audiences were going to fall asleep at a Deep Purple gig. Simper and Blackmore in particular concentrated hard on the visuals, and their experiences working with The Pirates and The Savages were now put to greater use in their own band. From the word go, it was apparent that Blackmore wanted to be the centre of attention on stage, but his self-confidence in his musical ability didn't always gain him new friends. During this first tour, Nick Simper recalls that they bumped into the Jeff Beck Group in Copenhagen and Blackmore's irreverence knew no bounds. Talking to Rod Stewart, and recalling the night at the Marquee a couple of month's earlier, Blackmore drew him in, hook, line and sinker when he commented to Stewart: "It was really great." Stewart apparently perked up, "yeah?" "Especially the bit when you went to the loo," Blackmore quipped, leaving the singer somewhat deflated. It was typical of Blackmore's attitude and would continue unabated forever more.

The tour included shows in Roskilde, The Nimb Club in Copenhagen and Gothenburg in Sweden. The material performed at these early shows consisted mainly of covers. Rod Evans's idea of The Beatles 'Help' as a ballad was included, as was The Rolling Stones' 'Paint It Black' performed instrumentally and used to showcase Ian Paice's drum solo. Hendrix's 'Hey Joe' was another well-known song that was thrown in for good measure, while Skip James's 'I'm So Glad' (also covered by Cream) and Joe South's 'Hush' helped to bolster the set. Some of the songs conceived during the two months at Deeves Hall were also included, most notably the two songs that Blackmore and Lord had jammed together during their first meeting in December '67: The instrumental 'And The Address' was used to open the show – an ideal number to allow the organist and guitarist to project their talents; while 'Mandrake Root' would soon develop into a number with lengthy improvisations.

For the new band the first tour was an unqualified success, and shows how easy it was in the sixties to launch a band, compared to today. John Coletta was pleased with the way it had gone: "We were very successful over there for two weeks. We really had a marvellous time, and we had television and radio, and for an unknown group with no record that was quite something. We got the booking over there by just phoning a promoter and telling them our problem. We just said, 'you know that we would like to bring this group over, and just wanted to cover our expenses,' we didn't care, we just wanted to get the experience in front of an audience. Mind you it cost us a few bob, because by the time we'd paid for the hire of a lorry and cars and transport and everything I suppose we lost two or three hundred pounds on that trip."

On returning to London the band were informed that two days of studio time had been booked over the second weekend of May at Pye's Marble Arch studios to record their first album.

EMI's decision to book only two days showed that they weren't prepared to spend much money on their new signings, but it was also a testimony to the quality of the musicianship that an album could be completed in such a short space of time. In effect they virtually performed live, playing the songs they had just performed on the short Danish tour. Most tracks were done in one take, although some were run through twice, with the best take being selected by Derek Lawrence who produced the sessions. Recording on four-track equipment didn't give much room for error: the drums and bass were recorded on the same track, an astonishing feat to comprehend in this day and age of massive multi-track facilities at the disposal of modern acts.

But if EMI expected the band to record in double-quick time, the same didn't apply when it came to releasing the album. EMI's casual approach to the record, and the band in general, meant that it was four months after Derek Lawrence presented the finished recordings that 'Shades Of Deep Purple' was released in the UK. In America the approach was very different. Once Tetragrammaton heard the album it was all systems go and they arranged to release the album a full two months ahead of EMI. On both sides of the Atlantic, a unanimous decision to release 'Hush' as the single in June did prove to be a highly beneficial move… at least as far as the Americans were concerned. Tetragrammaton promoted the single well. It was reported that one radio station played the song every hour, and within the first month of release it had notched up an astonishing 600,000 sales. For Edwards and Coletta it was a vindication of their commitment: "We really went in business-wise because we put the money there. If we'd been going in amateurishly we would not have spent the money, we'd just have tried to get it off the ground and use other people's money or no money," explained Coletta. But in Britain, sales were far less impressive. Despite some good reviews in the music press,

EMI's promotion seemed far less aggressive than that of their American counterparts.

The single soon drifted into obscurity, as it was apparent that EMI was focusing all its attention on The Beatles. The loveable Liverpool lads had by now created their own label, Apple, and at the end of July had recorded what would be the first release on the label, namely 'Hey Jude.' Consequently, EMI was gearing up for the forthcoming distribution, and Deep Purple didn't feature highly in the companies reckoning. Fortunately they could afford to ignore this faux pas as 'Hush' would eventually reach number four in the American Billboard 100 chart and went on to sell over one million copies. Tetragrammaton was delighted with its new band and, even before 'Shades Of Deep Purple' hit the US stores, the US label gave the band a healthy $250,000 advance to record its second album, which they needed to finish in time for their upcoming debut US tour booked for October.

Even though EMI didn't appear as enthusiastic about its new signing in comparison with its American counterpart, early inroads in exposure were attempted in England with a few radio sessions for the BBC, as well as a handful of gigs. The first radio session took place at the BBC's studio 1 in Piccadilly on 18th June. BBC sessions were relatively easy for Deep Purple to get, as their producer Derek Lawrence explained: "A few of the BBC producers thought that heavy rock was cool and did a series of sessions. The early Deep Purple ones I went along to, to supervise the sessions." Three songs were recorded at the first session, all from the album they had just recorded: 'Hush,' 'One More Rainy Day' and 'Help.' All sessions done for the BBC at this time were normally recorded live in one take and then broadcast later. It was a testimony to Deep Purple's talent that they could rattle numbers off in such a way, even if occasionally they would do a second take of some tunes. A second BBC session was done a week later, where once again they recorded

'Hush' and 'One More Rainy Day,' plus two other cover tunes: Neil Diamond's 'Kentucky Woman' and a much more obscure song called 'It's All Over.' Although 'Kentucky Woman' was soon to be recorded again for the second album, the other track was sadly never committed to vinyl.

In terms of concerts, Deep Purple's first gig on home soil was on 3rd August at the Lion pub in Warrington, hometown of their roadie Ian Hansford. Hansford arranged the gig and the band agreed to do it for nothing except travel expenses, food and accommodation. Deep Purple's home debut couldn't have been worse, as they were taken off before they finished their set. Unfortunately the venue was more used to dance music and Northern Soul, and Purple's loud, raucous rock wasn't to the liking of the pub regulars. Hansford also remembers Blackmore's attempt to impress the audience, with his visuals backfiring on him: "Ritchie was trying to be flash with his guitar and going up and down the frets with a cymbal and then threw the cymbal on the floor and cut right through the PA leads!"

Along with a few other gigs, the Warrington date was used as a warm-up for an appearance at the 8th National Jazz & Blues Festival held at Sunbury between Friday 9th and Sunday 11th August. Purple had the opening spot on the main stage on the Saturday evening, kicking off at 7.00 pm with a half-hour set. It was an impressive bill that included Joe Cocker, Tyrannosaurus Rex, Ten Years After, Jeff Beck, The Nice, Ginger Baker and Arthur Brown. The band got a paltry mention in the official festival programme, journalists largely ignored their set and Chris Welch's review in Melody Maker infuriated the band as they were totally ignored, with Welch claiming that Joe Cocker started the show. It has to be said that they received a lukewarm reception from the crowd, as festival goer Franz Murer recalled Purple's set: "This was very early and nascent Purple, a far cry from the heavy demon of later years, in fact they were more of a pop band than anything else, their set consisting mainly of covers. What did strike us as amusing was their stage clobber – purple satin shirts with frills for the instrumentalists and black satin for the vocalist – (apart from Lord who got to wear a psychedelic jacket) – very chic! They were playing numbers like 'Hush', which was the only song that really stands out in my memory – and very possibly 'Hey Joe,' 'I'm So Glad,' 'River Deep Mountain High' and Neil Diamond's 'Kentucky Woman' – all of which were featured in their set lists of the time. Pretty much a covers band. They were yet to find their own voice." As the opening act, the Sunbury Festival did the band no favours. Some recollections even claimed the band was booed off stage. "It was awful, we died a death. I think what we were doing was good it just didn't have anything to do with what anybody else was playing," is the way Lord remembers it. They followed up this far-from-spectacular-performance with a forty-five

minute set in one of the alternative marquee stages at 9.00 pm. Roger Drew, who had followed Ritchie Blackmore's career since his days in The Outlaws, caught the second performance and was much more impressed: "Apart from the main stage there were various marquees set around the site where the lesser-known bands were playing. I wandered into one as the next band was setting up, and immediately recognised the ace guitarist. I figured that they would be worth a look so I hung around. One of my better decisions! I believe this was one of the earliest Deep Purple gigs; it may have been the first. I can't remember the details of the set but I do remember that they were sensational and I became an instant fan and have followed their career ever since."

The success of 'Hush' in America may not have had a knock-on effect back in England, but column inches were given in the music press portraying Purple's Stateside success. When talking to Record Mirror, Jon Lord played down the band's instantaneous success, and explained how the band got together, though bizarrely without mentioning the names of the individuals who helped kick start Deep Purple: "it's an amazing series of coincidences and pure luck that's put us in our current position. I'd always had an idea of getting a group together of musicians who I thought were really good, and who I felt I could work with. Then one night a few months ago I was on my way to a gig – just going out of the front door of the house – when the phone rang. It was someone inviting me to a party. At the party I met someone not connected with the music scene and we got talking. He said he was interested in getting a good group together – and he asked me who I'd choose for the group if it were up to me. I told him and didn't think any more of it. A couple of days later I had a phone call from him telling me to go ahead and get the group together. That's basically how Deep Purple were formed."

Ian Paice explained to Melody Maker the thinking behind Deep Purple's music: "We try to incorporate classical music into pop. Our organist was trained as a classical pianist and he joins it all together. We all do the arrangements together and he supplies the classical knowledge. The result puzzles audiences who are expecting Sam and Dave stuff. They are taken aback at first and don't know what to make of it, but they soon catch on. As far as we are concerned dancing audiences are out. There are only about three numbers in our act that they can dance to. We make a point of warning promoters that we are not a dance group."

But even if the UK was proving to be a difficult market to break into, at least, thanks largely to their American benefactors at Tetragrammaton, they had a bit more time to make the second album. The recordings for this were done over a couple of weeks at De Lane Lea Studios. As Jon Lord told the press, "they gave us a big build up in America – but none of us expected this sort of success. The Tetra people sent over an advance of a quarter of a million dollars a few weeks ago for us to live on and use to record another album. They want to release it when we go over to America in October." The album followed a similar pattern to the first one, a mix of the band's own compositions and a few covers, including another stab at a Beatles tune, 'We Can Work It Out.' The extra time in the studio resulted in a more assured and improved sound, helped by the inclusion of more of their own songs, such as the album's opening cut, 'Listen, Learn, Read On,' and the superb instrumental 'Wring That Neck.' However, the end results were another record with a variety of styles that suggested that Deep Purple didn't really know in what direction it wanted to go. In fact the album was even more diverse than the first, and even included a string section on the ballad 'Anthem.' Although there was no denying the quality of musicianship, none of the band had much experience of composition, so it was often a case of throwing whatever they could come up with into the melting pot. As a result, despite the band's desire to play in the heavier, more aggressive style, Jon Lord's classical influences often conflicted with the visions that Simper and Blackmore were driving for.

Nevertheless, when the second album was completed it was released in America, not long after 'Shades Of Deep Purple' had been released in Britain. A second US hit single also followed in the shape of Neil Diamond's 'Kentucky Woman,' taken from the mysteriously entitled second album, 'The Book of Taliesyn.' With 'Kentucky Woman' once again getting plenty of airplay across the States, Purple embarked on its first US tour, starting at the huge LA Forum, supporting Cream. It had only been two years since Cream had first come on the scene, but they were now bowing out, and the original plan was for Purple to support them on their full American 'farewell tour;' however, these plans were aborted and Purple only joined the tour on 18th October, a fortnight after it had started.

With a top ten hit at their disposal, and a second single riding high, Purple weren't exactly unknowns and, following three successful gigs, they were quickly removed from the rest of the tour. Although the Cream camp didn't go into details for this, it was generally considered that Deep Purple were going down far too well with the audiences. Clapton in particular must have been looking over his shoulder, following his encounter with Blackmore a couple of years earlier. This was certainly the way Nick Simper saw things: "I can understand Eric Clapton not being too pleased. He must have known of Ritchie's reputation – not going to look too special following this bloke." Some suggested that it was the Purple guitarist's general irreverence to all and sundry that displeased Cream. During Blackmore's solos he often threw in some light-hearted moments such as 'God Save The Queen' or 'Jingle Bells.' But when interviewed in 2000, Jon Lord remembered events rather differently: "We got on well with them. They had no idea we were to be taken off the tour – they were too stoned!" Fundamentally, with one band on the way out and the other just embarking on the start of its career, it was to some extent academic, although in the short term it did mean that Purple had to organise some hastily arranged alternative gigs to justify the value of their trip to America.

With demand for the band increasing all the time, they remained Stateside until the beginning of the following year, touring America extensively from coast to coast. This was just as well because, despite the initial success in America, EMI still wasn't taking the band seriously. Despite re-issuing 'Hush' in September, the clamour for Deep Purple in its homeland was pretty non-existent. Since recording the first album, they had only done a handful of gigs before being whisked off to America, and EMI's decision to continually push The Beatles seemed rather odd, given that the 'Fab Four' were guaranteed to shift bucket loads of records however they were promoted. The initial trip to America concluded with four shows in New York City, including two at the prestigious Fillmore East. Partly because Deep Purple became an instant success, some critics astonishingly saw them as nothing more than a manufactured teenybopper group. This was all that the group needed to spur them on. The Fillmore crowds were renowned for being hostile if they spotted chinks in the armour. The ice was broken when Blackmore went to the front of the stage and played a very simple but fast run on his guitar. Merely the kind of note progression that he normally reserved for practising, it sounded really freaky, the audience loved it and from that point on the audience was won over.

Girlfriends flew over from England and joined the band in New York for Christmas. An astonishingly successful year was reviewed by all over a few drinks in their luxurious hotel accommodation. It was a world apart from the dingy flats and bed-sits they had been used to a year earlier. On returning to Britain in early January, their time in between gigs was spent back in the studio working on material for the third album, but, amazingly, EMI still hadn't even released 'The Book Of Taliesyn.' Although the band hadn't been together for a full year at this stage, when they started to record the new material, the album gelled together much more than the previous two LPs. Heavier numbers such as 'Chasing Shadows,' 'Bird Has Flown' and 'Why Didn't Rosemary?' were more indicative of the image Purple would soon carve out for itself worldwide. 'Why Didn't Rosemary?' in particular was an outstanding track, which according to the album's sleeve notes was inspired by an Otis Span number, although the riff is also identical to Elvis Presley's 'Too Much.' However, the soloing from Blackmore definitely left Elvis's guitarist, Scotty Moore, well and truly in the shade. Lyrically Rod Evans's vocals were inspired after the band had gone to the cinema one evening to watch the latest film called 'Rosemary's Baby' starring Mia Farrow. But even if the

majority of material on the album was heavier, once again Jon Lord couldn't help but introduce classical elements, this time going one step further than on the previous album, with both a full-blown string and woodwind section and a choir for the grandiose 'April.' This would prove to be a precursor to Purple's next project, but there would be major upheavals before this project got off the ground. By now the management team had been reduced to two after Edwards and Coletta bought out Ron Hire. In reality, Hire had been purely an investor and wasn't involved in the daily running of the band. With Hire having been charged with receiving stolen goods, and subsequently imprisoned, Edwards and Coletta moved swiftly to do a deal with Hire and buy out his share of the investment to avoid any bad publicity.

During the recording of the album, Blackmore pulled Lord to one side and expressed his dissatisfaction with Rod Evans's vocal performances, but the band continued working on the album throughout January, slotting in a few gigs around Britain in between sessions. Although Purple spent the early part of '69 back in the UK, the fees generated by concerts would only reach £150. In the States they could command fifteen times that amount, and a second US tour was booked to kick off on 1st April. Financially the tour would prove to be just as successful, although the costs of running the band were still outweighing the income. Simper in particular wasn't happy with what he saw as unnecessary and sometimes lavish expenditure, but behind the scenes Lord and Blackmore were becoming far more preoccupied with their increasing disillusionment with Rod Evans.

Before the recording of the third album had been completed, a new band had just released its self-titled debut album. Born out of the ashes of the Yardbirds, Jimmy Page's new outfit Led Zeppelin was an instant success in the UK, and Blackmore in particular was impressed with Zeppelin vocalist Robert Plant. In later years he claimed to have seen the band performing at Mothers Club in Birmingham, but Blackmore's memory must have been hazy because on the March evening in 1969 when Zeppelin played Birmingham, Purple were performing in Brighton. It's more likely that Blackmore caught the band in London, at one of the shows done later the same month, just before Purple departed for its second American tour. But such details are unimportant: Blackmore in particular had his mind set on a vocalist who could project his voice over a greater wall of sound, particularly if the band was going to compete with Zeppelin. Indeed, no sooner had Led Zeppelin's debut hit the stores when another new band from Birmingham also released its debut, self-titled album called 'Black Sabbath.' This too was harder and heavier than any of the material that Purple had just laid down at the De Lane Lea Studios in London.

With time always against them when recording, the albums didn't give a fair representation of what the band was like live; on stage the group's music was becoming heavier all the time, and Evans's vocal style didn't lend itself to the way they wanted the music to go. Nick Simper shared Lord and Blackmore's views: "Rod had met an American girl and got bitten by the Hollywood bug, and he had aspirations to be a film actor. I think he genuinely believed he was going to be a movie star. His singing definitely went down. He didn't seem bothered if he was singing flat or not." But there was no way they could replace Evans in the middle of an important American tour, so they soldiered on. Another factor that required consideration was whether or not they could get Paice and Simper to agree. If not, the decision would be a minority one and they wouldn't be able to make the desired change. Getting Ian Paice to agree could be potentially tricky as Evans had got him the gig in the first place. Would he now agree to see his mate kicked out of the band? The world of rock music can be ruthless at times, and during the tour Paice was pulled to one side and surprisingly agreed to Blackmore and Lord's plan, after which the decision was put to the management: "Ritchie and Jon came to me one day towards the end of the American tour and said they wanted to change when we got back to England," explained Coletta. "I said, 'oh well, if that's what you want to do, then let's wait until we get back; let's finish the tour, get back and sort it all out there.'" With a band majority and the management in the know, the search was on for a replacement on returning to England in early June.

- CHAPTER THREE-
HERE IN MY
DEEP PURPLE DREAMS

BLACKMORE CALLED Mick Underwood, his former band mate in both The Dominators and The Outlaws, in the hope that he might have a few suggestions. What Blackmore wasn't expecting was Underwood suggesting the lead singer of his own band! On leaving The Outlaws, Underwood had gone on to join The Herd and then The James Royal Set. Ironically, after a tour with the latter, Underwood was approached by Peter Grant, who he knew from the time when Grant had been tour manager for Gene Vincent with The Outlaws as his backing band. Grant had teamed up with Jimmy Page and was recruiting musicians for what would become Led Zeppelin. Underwood considered the offer, but instead chose to join Episode Six, an established act that had already cut several singles.

Before joining the band, Underwood already knew Episode Six's lead singer Ian Gillan, as both came from the same Hounslow area of West London. Ian Gillan was born at Chiswick Maternity Hospital on 19th August 1945 in Hounslow, London. Gillan had been in several bands in his local area during the early sixties, although none ever got any further than gigging. He also used several stage names in his early career. With his first band, The Moonshiners, Gillan went under the name of Garth Rockett, and while a member of his next outfit, The Javelins, he sometimes referred to himself as Jess Gillan or Jess Thunder. He then spent a year in a band called Wainwright's Gentlemen, and on his departure Brian Connelly replaced him.

It was May 1965 when he joined Episode Six. This turned out to be a positive career move, as soon after his appointment the band secured a record deal with Pye Records and the first of several singles was released in January '66. Episode Six also did several sessions for BBC Radio, and got gigs on some of the package tours of the day, including one with headliner Dusty Springfield.

By the time that Blackmore contacted Underwood, Episode Six had gone through several line-up changes, but they had failed to achieve the real breakthrough that would see the band move up another rung on the pop music ladder to ultimate success. On 4th June, Blackmore and Lord pitched up at Episode Six's gig at the Ivy Lodge Club in Woodford Green in North East London. Neither Ian Gillan nor any of the other band members had any reason to suspect that they were there to check anyone out, but merely assumed that they dug the band. Blackmore even got up on stage at one point and jammed with them, although the group didn't take too kindly to this. Mick Underwood remembered: "Ritchie got up and had a little play with us but at that time only Ian was in the frame as far as I knew but of course they took Roger as well, which was rather sad for Nicky. But he wasn't in the frame, nothing was mentioned about bass players, they just wanted another singer."

Gillan was promptly invited to a meeting with Blackmore and Lord. What happened over the next few days wouldn't have been out of place in the world of espionage. Three days after attending the Episode Six gig, a session was booked for Deep Purple to record a new single. Rod Evans was actually still in America. Having fallen in love with an American girl, he stayed on for a few days after the tour had finished to sort out his wedding arrangements. Blackmore, Lord, Simper and Paice went to the studio to lay down the backing tracks but, after a couple of hours, the session was knocked on the head.

Some cock and bull story was made up and told to Simper that the studio was unavailable in the afternoon, and that they would have to return in the evening. However, Lord, Paice and Blackmore returned with Ian Gillan, who also brought along Roger Glover, Gillan's bass playing colleague from Episode Six. "It was only pure luck that I wasn't at the studio when Ian Gillan arrived," says Simper. "Sources close to the band told me that I was going to be told Gillan was joining when I arrived for the session that evening. The roadie said when he went to pick up Gillan; Glover was with him and said he was coming for the ride. We'd been in there in the morning laying down backing tracks, if I was out of the band why did they go through all the motions and expense to do that? What I was told adds up because I was told we could only have the studio in the morning and in the evening so during the afternoon we had a break and I was told Gillan was going to be brought to the studio, taught the song, complete the routine, maybe even lay the vocal down, who knows and when I got there in the evening I would be told the truth."

There were two main reasons why such underhand shenanigans were going on. Firstly, they clearly didn't want Rod Evans to find out until the session was done. Also, Ian Gillan was under contract to the manager of Episode Six, so HEC was concerned about possible litigation. "It was all to be kept hush, hush," continues Simper. "According to people who were in the studio that night they decided, probably after an afternoon of jamming with uncle Roger on my equipment and my guitar that this worked out rather nice." The story Simper heard from the road crew proved to be true when, a few years later, Blackmore admitted that Glover hadn't been considered. "Roger turned up to the session to do one number we did. We weren't originally going to take him until Paicey said 'he's a good bass player let's keep him,' so I said 'okay.'"

Roger Glover was born in Brecon, South Wales on 30th November 1945, but he grew up in London, where his parents ran a pub. While at Harrow County school Glover joined his first band, the Madisons. A rival school band called The Lightnings also existed, and before long bassist Glover, along with fellow Madisons Tony Lander on guitar and the drummer, Harvey Shields, became part of The Lightnings. By October 1963 the band had opted for a name change and duly re-named themselves Episode Six. Following the replacement of vocalist Andy Ross with Ian Gillan, Glover slowly started to encourage the new singer to write lyrics to his song ideas.

By the time Deep Purple offered the gig to Gillan, they had seen the attraction of having Episode Six's bass player as well. The one thing that Purple had struggled with up to this point was composition, and getting a song writing team on board in the shape of two new members was an opportunity that Lord, Paice and Blackmore couldn't resist. Glover duly slotted in on the session, and the new five-piece knocked out a version of 'Hallelujah,' composed by the successful song writing team of Roger Greenaway and Roger Cook. This duo had already scored with hit records for Andy Williams, Cilla Black, Gene Pitney and Cliff Richard, amongst others, although it's fair to say that this list of middle of the road artists was definitely at odds with what Deep Purple were trying to achieve.

Nevertheless, the single was essentially aimed at the American market, and had been the brainchild of Tetragrammaton. For a b-side, the first part of the twelve-minute opus 'April' from the third album was used. As soon as the recording was completed, Gillan and Glover accepted the full time roles that were offered to them. However, they had to honour their existing gig bookings with Episode Six. Deep Purple also had some UK gigs scheduled and, three days after the session, with Evans and Simper still none the wiser, Deep Purple appeared in Cambridge playing the first of seven shows booked through June and July. More work was done on the 'Hallelujah' recording two days later with Gillan and Glover back in tow and, following a show in Birmingham on 14th June, the underhand shenanigans continued as Gillan and Glover joined Blackmore, Lord and Paice at Hanwell Community Centre in London, rehearsing and jamming ideas.

Eventually Nick Simper started to hear rumours that two new guys had been brought in to replace him and Rod Evans. Once he confronted the management they came clean, but explained that the decision was a majority one by the rest of the band. John Coletta explained that neither he nor partner Tony Edwards had any control over the decision. "I told them I couldn't do anything about it. I didn't have the right to hire and fire musicians ... that was the band's job," was the way he explained it to biographer Chris Charlesworth several years later. Although it had been left to the managers to break the news, years later Jon Lord openly admitted how poorly handled the situation was: "We got our management to call Rod and Nicky: Terribly cowardly thing to do. It's never a nice thing because it's a slight on what they hold dearest, which is their belief in their ability."

The original band concluded its schedule with a gig at Cardiff's Top Rank Ballroom on 4th July. Six days later, the new line-up debuted at London's Speakeasy Club. It was by no means a high profile event, and by all accounts wasn't exactly full to the rafters. "There were about twenty people there and they were all roadies apart from Keith Moon I think, who was under the table," is the way Gillan flippantly recalled it in his recent career documentary film. For Gillan and Glover, however, it was an unforgettable experience to be playing in a band with such accomplished musicians. For Gillan in particular, the opportunity to project his powerful voice over a much heavier backing than he was used to in Episode Six was a revelation. "Initially I was terrified, it was a big transition," recalled the singer a decade ago. Sheila Carter-Dimmock, Episode Six's keyboard player, conceded that it was somewhat inevitable: "Sooner or later someone was going to see this good looking guy with a great voice, oozing charisma and snap him up."

Although they had now secured the talents of two members of Episode Six, they had to get Gillan and Glover out of their contracts before the band could carry on without fear of litigation. "We had to break their contract, we had to pay a certain amount of money to the manager of the group, Gloria Bristow, to release them," said Coletta. "I think the group was breaking up anyway and had already got new ideas of what they wanted to do and everything, and so to her this was a little bit of a godsend, to get a little money for something she was already going to do. To us it was important so we paid up. I think it cost us £3,000 in the end, plus a lot of negotiations, but I think it paid off. I think you can say that was a good £3,000 spent. Immediately afterwards everything started to happen, even their playing fees went up from £125 to £350 to £400." Ironically Bristow used the £3,000 to help Episode Six drummer Mick Underwood to start up a new band, Quatermass. Once again, Underwood's band would prove to have an important bearing on future activities within Deep Purple, as will be revealed later in the story. The band also continued their regular rehearsals at Hanwell, working on new material during the days they had off between gigs. Fortunately for fans, some of the earliest shows by the new line-up were recorded. A gig at the Bilzen Jazz Festival in Belgium was filmed by Belgian TV, and the following night a gig at the Paradiso in Amsterdam was recorded for a radio broadcast.

Knowing that Deep Purple had already achieved success in America with hit singles and albums, and having familiarised themselves with Purple's sound, both Gillan and Glover were taken aback when it was announced that Jon Lord was writing a concerto to be performed at the Royal Albert Hall with The Royal Philharmonic Orchestra in late September. "Roger and I, being the new boys, were thinking, what's going on here? Are we in a rock band or a classical rock gimmick band? I showed a certain disrespect for the project," Gillan recently admitted.

When Jon Lord casually mentioned to Deep Purple's management his desire that one day he might compose a concerto for a rock band and orchestra, he didn't expect that they would be so keen that they would turn around a few weeks later and tell him they had booked the Royal Albert Hall, The Royal Philharmonic Orchestra and one of England's most respected composers and conductors in the shape of Dr Malcolm Arnold! The management's thinking might have appeared a bit odd, but as the concert was going to be for charity, it was bound to help raise Deep Purple's profile in its homeland. It was also arranged that the concert would be filmed and broadcast on TV, and this was an opportunity not to be missed. In some respects it turned out to be one of the most fortuitous decisions the band would make.

Although popularity up to this point had been concentrated in America, Tetragrammaton was starting to get into financial difficulties. Matters weren't helped when controversy arose on the third album's release. Called simply 'Deep Purple,' it first came out in the States just as the band was going through the line-up changes; but the major stumbling block was that the album's cover used a monochrome image of Hieronymous Bosch's fifteenth century artwork, 'The Garden Of Earthly Delights.' Tetragrammaton wasn't against such publicity. The previous year the label had agreed to release John Lennon's 'Two Virgins' album after Capitol Records had refused it because the cover depicted a full frontal nude photograph of Lennon and his girlfriend Yoko Ono. The Lennon album had been distributed in America with a brown paper bag over the cover. America always seems to throw up stark contrasts and, for a country that published the likes of 'Playboy' magazine, it seemed incredible that Deep Purple's album with a five hundred year old painting depicting naked people, which resides in Madrid's Prado Museum, should cause such outrage. However, some of the more puritanical States refused to display it publicly and, as a consequence, sales weren't a patch on what they had been for the first two albums. This merely added to Tetragrammaton's financial problems, which were mainly as a result of their own lavish spending and started to be manifested in deferred payments to the artists.

Meanwhile it looked like EMI might be starting to get its act together. A new label, Harvest, had been created to cater for the ever-growing trend for a more 'progressive' style of rock music. But it was still lagging behind in Purple's albums and had only just released 'The Book of Taliesyn.' Within just over a year, astonishing things happened to the band. From instant success in America, sales and demand for the band were already on the decline and, with upheavals in personnel, Deep Purple was at a crossroads. The new line-up desperately wanted to stamp its identity on the music scene, but Lord's agreement to his "concerto" project started to create new problems for the band. Blackmore in particular wanted to create an album that would stand up against anything produced by the happening bands of the day. There was just the small matter of the upcoming Royal Albert Hall performance to address.

With the management perhaps calling Lord's bluff, or maybe confident he could pull this off, the onus was on the keyboard player to start working on the project immediately. The fact that the project actually came to fruition at all was quite remarkable. The band couldn't afford the luxury of a few months break, so Lord started working on the composition in between gigs and rehearsals, but the others weren't too impressed with this. It meant extra work for Lord, slaving away on his manuscript at his Fulham flat while the other guys could afford to get a decent night's sleep after travelling back home from a gig. It also meant he missed band rehearsals and writing sessions for the material they were working on for the projected first album by the new line-up. Blackmore was the most outspoken critic of the situation, but the group had developed a writing pattern with the new boys. But while they jammed and worked out new ideas, they didn't take kindly to Lord being perceived by the press as the leader. Lord had always been the spokesman for the band, but the new writing partnership was unhappy with the press he was receiving about his forthcoming work.

Meanwhile, new songs developed quickly at rehearsals. The two earliest songs written by the new band would ultimately become two of their all-time classics. Originally called 'Kneel & Pray,' once the lyrics were completed, the first of these numbers that was designed as a set opener became know as 'Speed King.' The second was ironically one that stemmed from

a Jon Lord idea, although it was not an original one. According to rock critic Malcolm Dome, Lord was a close friend of Pattie Santos, vocalist with San Francisco band It's A Beautiful Day. The Purple guys had all heard the American West Coast group's debut album, and Lord in particular was drawn by the strings affect they used on an instrumental track called 'Bombay Calling.' Lord started to tinker with the melody, slowing it down, and with Ian Gillan adding some vocal lines over the top, before they knew it what would become the distinctive intro to 'Child In Time' had been created. Rehearsals continued in between 'one nighters,' but there was still the matter of Lord's upcoming "concerto" to deal with.

Although it was performed under the guise of Deep Purple, the "concerto" was to all intents and purposes a Jon Lord side project, or at least that seems to have been the original plan. It was during his days in The Artwoods that Lord initially had the idea of combining a rock band with an orchestra, after hearing the album 'Bernstein Plays Brubeck Plays Bernstein.' As he commented at the time, "if jazz can be combined with classical, why not rock?" However, Lord certainly wasn't original in uniting the two radically different fields. After all, there had been many artists in the early sixties who had adapted classical tunes into the popular music style of the day. For example, in 1961 Nero & The Gladiators created an adaptation of Edvard Grieg's 'In The Hall Of The Mountain King.' Coincidentally, Ritchie Blackmore had been in a short-lived group called the Lancasters who did a remake of this tune in 1965 and, the year before Lord's Concerto, Dave Edmund's band Love Sculpture had a big hit with its marvellous arrangement of Khachaturian's 'Sabre Dance.' But actually putting an orchestra and rock group on the same stage was an extremely new phenomenon, although Keith Emerson of The Nice had done just this a few weeks earlier at the Plumpton Festival with the LSO.

Although extensive rehearsal is vital to any new work, sufficient rehearsal time was not possible due to the costly nature of orchestras, and only three daily sessions were allocated before the big night. To make matters worse, many members of the orchestra considered it beneath themselves to play with a bunch of long-haired rock musicians, and the initial run through was, in Lord's own words, "an unmitigated disaster." Fortunately Lord had the full backing of Dr Arnold, and it wasn't until the well-spoken and mild-mannered Arnold shocked the orchestra by calling them "a bunch of cunts" that they finally got their act into gear. At the final rehearsal Arnold said to the Orchestra, "tonight we are going to make history. We may as well make music at the same time." Fortunately by the time of the premiere the whole thing had gelled together.

In general the show was a great success and most of the press reviewed it favourably. Having the opportunity to play a half hour set of their own material before the "concerto" was also a bonus for those who were present, although sadly the cameras weren't rolling as they performed 'Hush,' 'Wring That Neck' and the new composition, 'Child In Time,' which received its premiere at this prestigious event. In recent years, Jon Lord has been open enough to say that, "the musicians were obliged to play and some of them hated it! And even the people in the audience weren't all that thrilled. But it was 1969! But I think everything one does is a product of its time. Some things in this "Concerto" were really very much dead weight - I'd be the first to admit it but it was only an experiment. I only wanted to try and break these boundaries that separated rock 'n' roll from classic. On the other hand I don't want to reject anything I once did afterwards; I can now only look at some thing from an, if you like, 'wiser' perspective. I mean, nowadays "concerto" sounds somewhat old-fashioned, but that doesn't change the fact that it was important at the time.

And, to be honest, I still like it - the melodies, Gillan's singing, Ritchie's angry guitar, the whole atmosphere. I wouldn't distance myself from this."

But even if musically some may have raised their eyebrows at the event, the publicity Purple gained from that one evening in the UK was arguably more than they had received over the past year. In the short term, this extra publicity would also prove to present its own problems. "The next day the papers were full of us and Jon Lord suddenly became the main composer of the band, which really got up the noses of everyone else in the band, and Ritchie in particular felt very bitter about it," recalls Glover. Whilst the publicity inevitably introduced many new fans to the group, aside from the internal disharmony, another drawback was that so many people now saw Deep Purple as a band that played with orchestras. One infamous incident occurred a month after the performance when the band turned up in Ipswich for a gig, only to be told by the promoter that he couldn't book an orchestra, but had managed to secure the services of a brass band instead! Fortunately Deep Purple didn't actually play alongside them; however, the brass band performed as the opening act for what must rank as one of the more bizarre concerts the band has ever played.

Furthermore, as a direct result of the exposure, Jon Lord was thrust further into the limelight as the supposed leader and principal composer, causing greater friction between him and the band's principal writers. The public didn't know that the band was working on material for a new album, and Blackmore knew that most of the ideas were his and Glover's. Although he had only been in the band for a very short while, Glover had been brought in for his writing abilities and had already contributed heavily to songs that would feature on the next studio album. One of the band's road crew, Ian Hansford, observed that, "it came across as Jon Lord was the main songwriter. I know

Roger was pissed off with it." As Lord himself said, "the rest of the band were not amused but if there was any jealousy as such, I believe it stemmed mostly from Ritchie." The friction became so bad for a while that it left Lord feeling ostracised and he seriously considered quitting the band. Fortunately for all concerned the situation was amiably resolved, but it did result in Jon Lord taking a back seat from this time on.

The new material being recorded was coming on in leaps and bounds. Roger Glover remembered: "I went to this rehearsal hall and picked up the guitar and started playing something, and someone else started playing and I thought, I don't know this song, but neither did they. It was just a jamming band." Blackmore was clearly the main architect of the new direction: "I said: 'Jon, we should make a rock 'n' roll record for people in parties. It should be non-stop, hard-hitting rock 'n' roll.'" Furthermore, the live performances were improving all the time. The bulk of the live set was still based around the earlier material, and Gillan and Glover had to learn plenty of the back catalogue. A full show in Montreux, Switzerland was recorded and languished in the vaults for decades before being released in 2003 under the title 'Kneel & Pray.' Only two new songs found there way into the set: 'Child In Time' and the new set opener 'Kneel & Pray,' which soon became known as 'Speed King' once the lyrics were re-written. The remainder of the set was made up of 'Hush,' 'Wring That Neck,' 'Paint It Black,' 'Mandrake Root' and 'Kentucky Woman.' 'Bird Has Flown' from the third album was done for a BBC Radio session, but relying on so many of the older songs wasn't a big issue at this early stage. In fact for Ian Gillan it was more of a pleasure than a chore: "I was a fan of the band before I joined. Those albums were fantastic. I played them to death before I got the gig."

Even though they hadn't yet developed enough new material for a serious revamping of the set list, the time was ripe for musical experimentation. Looking back, Ian Gillan said, "The timing was perfect. The public was ready to move on with the wonderful flavour of what had gone before with The Small Faces, The Kinks & The Beatles. They wanted to hear the freedom and accept new ideas." With the musicianship within Deep Purple, they were ideally suited to be at the forefront of this dynamic change. Numbers such as 'Wring That Neck' and 'Mandrake Root' were now often stretched to thirty minutes or more as Blackmore and Lord displayed their virtuosity and wonderful talent for improvisation. The musical styles incorporated also knew no boundaries. Both players were familiar with classical and jazz music, and music from classical composers from Bach to Grieg would often find its way into the improvisations. Blackmore's interest in jazz players such as Wes Montgomery would also be employed during the mellower moments of 'Wring That Neck.' With the exception of Keith Emerson's The Nice, there weren't too many bands on the scene in late 1969 that would incorporate such diversity into their playing, but at the same time produce an overall sound so powerful that the listener was left with a feeling akin to standing next to a jet plane taking off!

Visually the band was also impressing reviewers and fans alike. During the long instrumental sections, Ian Gillan would play conga drums, with his ever-growing hair swirling around in time to the music. Jon Lord had originally started his career by performing seated at the organ, but soon added more aggression into his playing, attacking the organ with venom, rocking it back and forth and adding those marvellous crashing chord sounds that would become as much a hallmark of Deep Purple as Blackmore's dexterous, yet highly vicious guitar sound. Blackmore always had a head start on the rest of the band as far as showmanship was concerned, and he was also hell bent on being the star of the show. Like his contemporaries,

Pete Townshend and Jimi Hendrix, he too started laying waste to guitars and amps during the finale number of 'Mandrake Root,' while strobe lighting effects left the audience looking on in astonishment. When Ian Gillan joined the band, Blackmore took him to one side and stressed the point that he intended to blow him off stage with his performances. It was an approach that the rest of the band also adopted and musical battles developed nightly.

EMI eventually released the third album a couple of months after the Albert Hall gig. It was by this time totally out of vogue with what Deep Purple were doing and bore no resemblance to the new line-up. Just as the band was trying to forge a new direction, developing the new album and stage show, it seemed that one distraction after another was cropping up. Jon Lord's Concerto wasn't the only thing to deviate from the group's main intentions. Although Tetragrammaton originally released the recording of the Concerto in late '69, it soon disappeared without trace. Tetragrammaton's financial problems finally got the better of them and the company went into liquidation. This was a terrible blow for the band as access to their biggest market was temporarily put on hold while the situation was sorted out. EMI released the Concerto in the UK in January 1970, but what had been enjoyable as a one-off witnessed by thousands on TV didn't transcend into huge album sales.

By April the recordings for the new studio album were completed. The album had seen a writing pattern in which original ideas had normally come from Blackmore and Glover. The latter was also often involved with the lyric writing alongside Ian Gillan. Jon Lord and Ian Paice's input was minimal in truth, but it was agreed from the outset that all songs would be credited as group compositions. The decision had been made following some bickering in the original line-up. Blackmore in particular was taken aback by how much Rod Evans made for writing the lyrics to 'One More Rainy Day,' the b-side to the million selling 'Hush.' The decision to agree the five-way writing credits initially satisfied all concerned, but it would present its own problems as time went on. Blackmore and Paice had by now also got involved in an all-star jam session produced by Derek Lawrence. This included two guitarists greatly admired by Blackmore, Albert Lee and Big Jim Sullivan. Others included were Tony Ashton from Ashton Gardner & Dyke and two of Blackmore's former band mates: Matthew Fisher had played alongside Blackmore in the Savage before going on to huge fame as the organist on Procul Harum's iconic 'Whiter Shade of Pale;' bassist Chas Hodges had worked alongside Blackmore in The Outlaws, but is now more well known as one half of Chas & Dave! It was somewhat ironic that Blackmore and Paice agreed to the session, as Lawrence had just been removed from his position as Deep Purple's producer. For the new album the band had elected to self-produce. Due to contractual reasons, the artists involved in the new project couldn't be named, the 'Green Bullfrog' album sunk without a trace and the original release is now a prized collector's item.

Further distractions were to raise their ugly heads: The success that had greeted the Concerto in some quarters resulted in Lord being commissioned by the BBC to do another work combining a rock group and an orchestra, once again to the particular mortification of Blackmore. Fortunately this wasn't scheduled for several months and, with the American market temporarily on hold, the band had no option but to put all their attention into the European market. For the first few months of 1970 the band would embark on an extensive bout of touring in Britain and mainland Europe, developing a reputation for stupendous live performances. Surprisingly very little of the new material had been added to the set. 'Speed King' had already been established as the set opener within a few weeks of Gillan and Glover joining, and 'Child In Time,' which had debuted at the Albert Hall event, was soon establishing itself as a concert classic. But other than these, 'Wring That Neck,' 'Paint It Black' and 'Mandrake Root' continued to form the cornerstone of the live act. In truth, due to the lengthy improvised performances each night, there wasn't really much space for additional songs.

Although an album's worth of material was now in the can, the management team wanted a single. Even though the band's first success had been achieved this way, the developing trend of 'progressive' rock music generally saw singles as inconsequential. Led Zeppelin in particular would vehemently refuse to make singles, and elsewhere much of the material that many bands within the genre were producing was either too long or too uncommercial to even consider for singles. Deep Purple wasn't exactly against the idea, but hadn't really given much thought to it. This probably explains why, when they went back into the studio at the management's request, they didn't take the session too seriously. With very little in the way of ideas developing, the lads temporarily abandoned the session for a bit of liquid refreshment at the local pub. On their return, somewhat the worse for wear, Blackmore struck on the idea of using the bass riff from Ricky Nelson's rocked up interpretation of George Gershwin's 'Summertime.' The track had been the b-side of 'Young World,' a moderate hit for Nelson in 1962. Within an hour or so, a song had been knocked into shape. Gillan and Glover took the title of an old Arthur Alexander song 'Black Night' as the basis for the lyrics. In their drunken state, they tried to come up with something as banal as possible. After completing the track, none of the guys gave it a second thought but the management loved it. They'd got their single, much to the bemusement of the band.

The early part of 1970 also saw negotiations in America to untangle the mess made by Tetragrammaton's demise. Warner

Brothers acquired its back catalogue and roster of artists, which would eventually work out to Deep Purple's advantage. Warner inherited the band and, in doing so, began to sort out the back dated royalties with an initial payment of $40,000. Warners chose not to re-issue any of the albums with the exception of the 'Concerto For Group And Orchestra' and, as a way of helping to promote it, it was somewhat reluctantly agreed to perform this at the Hollywood Bowl with the Los Angeles Philharmonic Orchestra. The following year, John Coletta explained what happened with Tetragrammaton: "The record company went bankrupt and of course we had all these royalties which we weren't going to get and the market of course was dead. We couldn't move out of the contract because although they were really bankrupt they didn't go bankrupt, they called a moratorium of their creditors and it was held off until they could find somebody to buy over the existing contract, and there was some film rights and things like this which Warner Brothers had given them. That took us about eighteen months to get out of that, which lost us eighteen months in America and we had to come back to England. So there was no product out in the States and no market here because we weren't big enough here. We were getting sort of £125 a night, so we had to come back and really go to work on the European market, it was our only hope. We did and we worked bloody hard and we came back and did the concert at the Albert Hall with the orchestra. We needed something to get them to the front and we thought that's the way to do it. The group didn't basically want to do it because they felt it was diverting, diverging too far from the rock field, which it was in a way, but I don't think it did them any harm at all. In the long run it did them a lot of good."

Although Purple's popularity was on the up, it would still be quite a while before they were regularly playing the larger venues, and the clubs and universities still formed the majority of gigs. On 12th June they played at the Eel Pie Island Club in Twickenham, South London, situated in the middle of the River Thames. Due to the amount of equipment that Deep Purple had, they were unable to get their truck over the narrow bridge. The venue was used to this and was prepared for the problem. They supplied a couple of Morris Minor Travellers, so Deep Purple's roadies had to unload their truck and transfer all the gear across the bridge in the cars. But the gig is best remembered by roadie Ian Hansford because of Blackmore's unusual behaviour: "When we got there it was flooded, the floor was awash, The Thames must have been really high, and he played the set in the changing room," says Hansford. "He said to me, 'go and put a bit more top on the amp.' I can remember Jon Lord was furious, 'get him out here.' 'It's no good Jon, if I asked him to get out here is he going to say yes?' He might have started on stage but then he disappeared. I would say it was at least for three quarters of the set."

It wasn't the first time Blackmore's actions had angered his band mates, but it was certainly one of the most bizarre. What on earth the crowd thought of it all sadly, as far as is known, hasn't been documented. Looking back now it's easy to have a snigger, picturing Blackmore pounding out Purple classics such as 'Child In Time' and 'Mandrake Root' while sitting in the dressing room, but the band didn't take such a jovial view of Blackmore's behaviour. Roger Glover says, "I learnt quite early on he was going to do things for himself and no one else mattered."

In June the new album was finally released and soon became a huge success. 'In Rock' hadn't been an easy album to make. The band always preferred to spend an allocated time within the studio, but due to the financial problems they were incurring they had to continually gig to keep the money rolling in. Despite being recorded sporadically over several months, 'In Rock' was in fact the most cohesive and powerful album the band had produced. The album's title was important and was a deliberate message to anyone who mistook the band as a novelty act that dabbled with orchestras. With the previous release having been 'In Concert' (with an orchestra), the public was left in no doubt about what this album was all about. The album entered the UK charts instantly, eventually reached number 4 and would remain on the charts for well over a year. It was the first album that really forged an identity for the band. Jon Lord says: "We

believe in experimentation and excitement within the framework that we have set ourselves at this particular moment in time. That will change ... we will extend, obviously. We'll get older, get different influences; we've not reached a point where we are perfectly happy and contented to develop naturally. We were trying to develop un-naturally before. We would grasp all sorts of different ideas at once ... like a child in a garden full of flowers; he wants them all at once. When Ian and Roger joined, something very nice happened within the group."

New vocalist Ian Gillan drew much of the attention with his astonishing vocal abilities. Rock had its fair share of excellent and popular front men. No one could ignore the Rolling Stones' Mick Jagger; Free had the bluesy, soulful Paul Rodgers; Black Sabbath the inimitable Ozzy Osbourne; and Zeppelin's Robert Plant had been the catalyst for Blackmore's desire to change singers in the first place. But none could match the power and range of Ian Gillan. Even before 'In Rock' had been released, Tim Rice and Andrew Lloyd Webber had heard the recording of 'Child In Time.' Impressed with Ian Gillan's soaring vocals they approached him to take the lead role in 'Jesus Christ Superstar,' the new rock opera they had composed. Gillan agreed to do the studio recording and laid down all his vocal parts in just a few hours. It was a minor distraction, but the album went on to huge global success, significantly raising Ian Gillan's stature in the process.

The rest of the band also received their fair share of plaudits. Roger Glover's bass playing was solid, but his writing contributions were of equal importance with this. Jon Lord's Hammond playing was matched only by Keith Emerson, while Ian Paice was fast developing a reputation as one of England's finest drummers. For Ritchie Blackmore, after nearly ten years as a professional musician, he finally started to receive recognition for his immense talents on the six-string. August saw the band return to play at the National Jazz & Blues Festival, now relocated at Plumpton. Unlike two years earlier, Purple's set now met with huge favour from the crowd. The running order for the last night of the weekend was supposed to conclude with Yes, followed by Purple, with Juicy Lucy closing the show. With Yes turning up late, Purple had to go onstage before them; Blackmore was determined to make this a spectacle to remember, and during the climactic ending to 'Mandrake Root' he instructed roadie Ian Hansford to set fire to the amps, although the stage backcloth also went up in flames. As Melody Maker described in its report of the event, "guitars were flung around stage in wild abandon." One member of the audience recently recalled, "maybe my memory is going but I do seem to remember Deep Purple setting fire to the stage because the organisers wouldn't let them play on into Juicy Lucy's slot although they hadn't turned up. I'm probably wrong on this score, but the rumour on the street at the time gave this as one reason for the festival moving to Reading." In what would become a typical response for Blackmore, he merely retorted, "actually we meant to set the whole stage alight. I couldn't get in tune so I just threw the guitar wildly out."

By August 'Black Night' also entered the singles charts and was a massive success. It reached number two and was only held off the number one spot by Freda Payne's 'Band Of Gold.' After more than two years in the British wilderness and with a change of personnel, Deep Purple had finally made the breakthrough in its homeland. Who can say whether or not the breakthrough would have come at all if it wasn't for the problems they encountered in America? But the months of hard work and relentless concert performances back home had paid dividends at last. TV appearances raised the group's profile even more. The band was given a half hour slot by Granada TV on the 'Doing Their Thing' show, and London Weekend

Television broadcast a stupendous, albeit edited, twelve-minute performance of 'Mandrake Root' as part of its 'South Bank Summer.' Ian Gillan told Melody Maker, "we hadn't wanted to do television before; with all the hassles and three minute spots playing to back tracks but the South Bank thing was great. The other groups played to back tracks but we took all our gear and played live." It was the perfect advert for the rawness of Deep Purple's live performances. Recorded at the Queen Elizabeth Hall, the breathtaking finale saw Blackmore pulling out all the stops, while Ian Paice kicked over his drum kit as the song concluded. This prompted criticism in the music press by some who didn't take kindly to bands manhandling their equipment, but Ian Paice retorted by saying, "I bought it so I'll bloody well boot it!"

Blackmore was fast becoming recognised as one of Britain's finest guitarists. Eric Clapton, the man who had been ridiculously proclaimed "God" by his fans had at this point drifted into temporary semi-obscurity following the short-lived band Blind Faith. A month after Purple's success at the Plumpton Festival Jimi Hendrix, arguably the most influential guitarist of his generation, died in London in September 1970 after asphyxiating on his own vomit. There were few players on the scene, if any, to equal Blackmore's combination of technique, speed and showmanship, and the world was fast becoming his oyster.

But while this was all kicking off back home the reverse was now happening in America. The new album was now released in the States some considerable time after its UK counterpart. Furthermore, Warner Brothers initially appeared to have little understanding of exactly what type of band they had inherited. Years later, Jon Lord recalled the rather intense business meetings they had with Warner's executives: "how do you conceptualise this Jon?" is an example of the kind of questions they were confronted with around the table. All Deep Purple knew was that they had produced a mighty fine album that at last they could be truly proud of. The visit to America in August 1970 wasn't a happy one. Incredibly the band had already been largely forgotten by the hordes who had bought 'Hush' two years earlier, and they were back to square one. But with one market temporarily on ice, the clamour for the band in Europe was growing all the time. The phenomenal success of 'In Rock' and 'Black Night' had suddenly catapulted Deep Purple into the rock public's consciousness. In the same month, Lord's second orchestral piece 'The Gemini Suite,' which had been commissioned by the BBC, was performed at the Royal Festival Hall by Deep Purple along with the Light Music Society Orchestra, once again with Malcolm Arnold as the conductor. There was less publicity this time, no doubt pleasing both Gillan and Blackmore who clearly wanted to focus on rock 'n' roll. The performance was recorded and broadcast on BBC Radio, and was eventually released on CD in 1993.

Away from the distraction of further orchestral dabbling, the rest of the year saw the band touring relentlessly throughout the UK and Europe, and further appearances on TV were made, including the BBC's Top Of The Pops. "It cured us of looking down our noses at hit singles because the change in our public profile was dramatic," said Glover. September and October focused on the UK and France, where the band also appeared on TV performing a devastating set in Paris. For anyone who has witnessed this performance on 'Pop Deux,' the arrogance of youth is superbly illustrated with Blackmore drinking a bottle of beer while soloing one handed; and at one point during one of Jon Lord's solos, he entices a young fan from the audience to take over, holding down a one note drone on the Hammond organ while Lord takes a brief breather, with both the crowd and the astonished additional organist mesmerised by the experience. Purple could do no wrong, and the self-belief and confidence displayed on stage ensured the legion of fans was destined to keep growing at a staggering rate.

A four-date Scottish tour in October saw headlines in the papers such as "Purple Mania" and "Deep Purple Fans Fever" after dramatic events in Glasgow. Such was the demand for tickets that the gig was switched from the 1,000-capacity Electric Garden to the larger Tiffany's. However, in Britain in the early seventies, there were very few large, indoor venues that were big enough to cater for the demand and trouble erupted as thousands fought to get into the venue. Seventeen police cars and vans were called to the scene resulting in the headline, "3,000 pop fans in riot at hall door," in the following morning's Daily Record. Following the last of the four Scottish gigs in Dundee, the band travelled south for the next show at Sunderland's Top Rank Suite. It was a double header with Free, another of the new breed of British bands riding on a crest of a wave following its smash hit single 'Alright Now.' In fact, although co-headliners Free had been scheduled to go on last, Purple turned up late. In a role reversal from what had happened a couple of months earlier at Plumpton, Free took to the stage first. Free's lead singer Paul Rodgers was from the North East, so there was probably a greater representation of Free fans in the venue. Even though the show was billed as not finishing until two in the morning, Purple had actually decided they had got there too late to perform and went straight to their hotel instead. The promoter was having none of it and phoned them up, explaining that Free had already played and 3,000 fans were desperately waiting to see them. The 'Purple Mania,' as it had been labelled in Scotland, was also having an effect south of the border. Roger Glover explained to Melody Maker that, "there were worse scenes in Sunderland. I think either of us could have sold the place out. Girls were flinging themselves at Ian and we played 'Black Night' to the backs of bouncers. Girls were fainting, crying and screaming, and they were laying them at our feet on the stage. They were screaming for the wrong reasons. It wasn't the music that we played; it was just what we looked like that counted because they were all very young. I suppose it's something we will have to face after appearing on Top Of The Pops."

Three gigs in Scandinavia in mid-November included a show at the Konserthuset in Stockholm, recorded by Swedish Radio. Deep Purple fans are fortunate that enterprising radio stations saw fit to record concerts for broadcast, and this show in particular is as good an example as one could get of Deep Purple's live act at that time. The tapes were originally released in 1988 as the album 'Sandinavian Nights,' with a much-improved, re-mastered, re-titled 'Live In Stockholm 1970' coming out in 2005. By necessity, 'In Rock' had been recorded over several months as a result of spending as much time as possible touring and building up a worthy live reputation. In November Glover told Sounds, "I don't think this one will take as long as 'In Rock.' We'd like to finish it in February to release it in March". However, because 'In Rock' was such an overwhelming success, the knock-on effect was a greater demand for concert performances. As a consequence, the recording sessions for the follow up album continued in a similar fashion, but proved to take even longer to produce. In fact, nine months passed from the time the band first entered the studio to work on it to the point of its completion. Bear in mind that these were the days when it was the norm for bands to put out albums at much more frequent intervals than today. Indeed, Deep Purple had released its first five albums between September '68 and June 1970: five albums in under two years! The recording for what would become 'Fireball' had started in September at London's De Lane Lea Studios, but only one track was laid down at this session. 'Anyone's Daughter,' a country flavoured, laid back number was highly untypical of anything produced for 'In Rock.' The band was struggling to come up with ideas, as Glover explained to New Musical Express the following year: "We were sitting around the studio waiting for inspiration and Ritchie just started tinkling around with that chord thing and we joined in. It was a fun number."

As the year was drawing to a close, Roger Glover commented to one magazine that he was still confident the album could be released by March. Ian Gillan also told Disc magazine in November, "Ritchie and I wrote a couple of songs the other night. Two tracks are virtually complete. It shouldn't take so long this time because we know more about recording techniques." Nothing could be further from the truth, and writing and recording were put on hold as demand for touring continued unabated.

The last gigs of the year were in Germany, another country that had really taken Purple to its hearts and to this day is a stronghold for the band. However, it wasn't all love and kisses at the gig in Lüdenscheid. Blackmore had been taken ill and airlifted back to England, and the band agreed to perform as a four piece. Without Blackmore's guitar driving the songs along, they nevertheless did a sterling job with a shortened set of around an hour. While it would be perfectly understandable if the audience felt disappointed by the lack of guitar, the demand for an encore was in fact as great as ever. The band didn't feel that they could do anymore without Blackmore and promptly went back to their hotel, but the crowd was having none of it and stormed the stage, smashing equipment and causing thousands of pounds of damage. As Jon Lord explained, "some git got up on stage and said that we would be back in an hour to play for two more hours. The roadies had to flee through the backstage toilet window otherwise they'd have been torn apart from the mob." Fortunately as the riot was a direct result of the stage announcement, the band managed to sue the local council for the cost of the damage to their equipment. Blackmore's illness was short-lived and he returned for the next gig in Stuttgart, but the news of the riot in Lüdenscheid had spread throughout the country and when the band arrived at the venue the guys were amazed to see that the army had been brought in to prevent possible further rioting. Three separate crash barriers had also been erected in front of the stage, one of them with barbed wire! Roger Glover said: "I remember sitting in the dressing room thinking, all this going on just so five of us can get up to play some music. After the show it took us two hours to drive half a mile back to our hotel. We knew we'd made it that night."

The Stuttgart gig on 12th December concluded not only an eventful tour, but also an astonishingly eventful year on the road. There was just enough time before a well-earned break over Christmas to do further work on the next album. For the first time since the band had got together at Deeves Hall they made a conscientious decision to spend some dedicated time writing. A remote farmhouse in Devon known as the Hermitage was picked as an ideal location to lock themselves away for a fortnight and work on new ideas. Roger Glover explained the thinking behind this: "We thought it would be nice to cut ourselves off completely so that we could work away at new material without any distractions at all." However, little progress was made and it was treated more as a holiday than anything else. The band was exhausted from the recent spate of work and spent most of the time in the local pubs, and, in Blackmore's case, indulging in one of his favourite pastimes, séances. The period also saw the start of some petty in-fighting, which often disrupted the work. Ian Gillan's heavy drinking wasn't endearing him to the rest of the band, particularly Blackmore, and the start of a personality clash developed. Glover recalled: "Ian seemed to go off the rails with attitude and drinking problems. I've searched my memory to try and work out why he went down that route. He and Ritchie were at complete loggerheads." From the outset of the band Blackmore had always adopted a selfish approach. As roadie Ian Hansford recalls, "if he didn't want to do anything he wouldn't do it. He wouldn't even consider the band, 'I'm not doing it.' As simple as that: Very selfish." Such an attitude clearly affected Ian Gillan more than the rest of the band. "Ian may have got to the point where he thought, I'm the singer of the band – if Ritchie can behave like that so can I," said Glover. "Looking back it was a time when various frictions within the band began to grow. What were niggles during the In Rock period started to become part of band life. It wasn't an entirely happy period," concluded Glover. Even the generally congenial bassist lost his rag one night in Devon, when Blackmore smashed an axe through Glover's bedroom door. Glover chased Blackmore through the house and eventually found him cowering in a corner, but wisely decided not to carry out the murder he had initially contemplated when he leapt out of bed!

There was little opportunity to welcome in the New Year in the traditional style as 1st January saw gigging recommence in Rotterdam. A lengthy UK tour kicked off in Leeds Town Hall towards the end of the month and went through to Aberdeen Music Hall on 8th March. Bill Hicks, a reader of the author's More Black than Purple publication, caught the show in Glasgow at Greens Playhouse. In fact, Hicks remembers the problems encountered when Purple had played Glasgow the previous October: "Suffice to say that, due to 'In Rock' having just been released, the venue was too small, the concert was switched to a larger one a few doors away and there was a near riot of would-be fans wanting to get in. But I wasn't one of them because, having been entrenched in Eddison Lighthouse, Middle Of The Road and all the other rubbish that was in the charts at that

time, I had yet to see the light. And that came about when a mate played me a track from a Harvest label sampler album called 'Picnic A Breath Of Fresh Air' which contained Into The Fire. From the moment I heard da da da-da-da-da I was hooked, though it was too late for the Electric Garden."

Like so many young rock music fans, Hicks was now bitten by the bug and was anxious to see Deep Purple: "So some months later it was off to an electrical retail shop which had a ticket office, in Sauchiehall Street, as it happens, to fork out my 21 shillings (£1 10p if you're too young to remember) for my Purple ticket. The venue for this gig was Greens Playhouse which had a place in the history books as once being the largest cinema in Europe and it went on to become the world-famous Glasgow Apollo. I remember some of it as though it was yesterday, yet other parts of it have disappeared into the depths of my brain never to see the light of day again. At the tender age of 15, my mate George Carroll and I were over the moon that Deep Purple were heading to Glasgow for the second time in as many months. When we arrived it was the first time I'd ever been in the place and to this day I can still visualise the sight of the 15-foot high stage, along with Ritchie's stack of Marshalls off to the right-hand side, which seemed miles away from where we entered. The support band? Nope, I can't remember who they were, but I distinctly recall Purple hitting the stage, Gillan in pink T-shirt and denims. As soon as the first chords crashed out over the thousands of heads everyone was mesmerised. 'Wring That Neck,' 'Black Night,' 'Child In Time,' 'Lucille,' 'Mandrake Root' and possibly 'Speed King' were all there, but it was just too overwhelming for a 15-year-old former pop lover to take in. The volume was unbelievably high and the fleas – Greens had seen better days – that bred, lived and fed off patrons were surely slaughtered by the wailing solos from the Man in Black, the screams of Mr Gillan and the pounding bass and drums of Glover and Paice. In those days, of course, long solos were the order of the day and, being a naive youngster, I assumed those not on stage sat in the dressing-room or wings waiting for their turn to come. What did I know about rock singers having a bonk under the piano and such things? The vision of Ritchie wielding his Strat, crashing it on to the floor of the stage, into the side of the speakers and finally throwing the broken pieces into the lions' den was too much to bear and took on an almost haunting air under the flickering strobe. As for Ian Paice, I was truly worried about him. I remember thinking that if my mother saw him she'd be saying something like, 'That young man will have a heart attack or catch his death if he goes out into the cold air!' But it really was the Man in Black who captured everyone. After that Greens gig, I couldn't wait for 'Fireball' to be released, head for the concert venue again and repeat what had gone before."

The tour used several support acts, most of which featured former associates and friends. Ashton, Gardner & Dyke supported on the first few shows, and Tony Ashton was an old friend of Jon Lord's. The pair collaborated on several projects as the years progressed. Heads, Hands & Feet included Blackmore's former band mate from The Outlaws, bassist Chas Hodges, and Albert Lee, both of whom he had worked with the previous year on the 'Green Bullfrog' sessions. Perhaps as a result of the never-ending workload, the tour was also beset with illness as Roger Glover suffered with severe bouts of acute stomach pains. At some shows the pain was so bad that Glover was unable to go back on stage for the encores, and Chas Hodges deputised when required. The duo Hardin & York, who also supported at some shows, would also crop up in projects involving various members of Purple at regular intervals during the next few years. In fact a mere three days after the end of tour Aberdeen gig, Lord, Paice and Glover all appeared on stage at an all-star jam session organised by Hardin & York at Bumpers Club in London. Other musicians who appeared included Ray Fenwick, Miller Anderson, Mick Weaver, Dee Murray, Keith Moon and Keef Hartley. Ian Paice also played alongside Pete York on a number called 'Extension 345' during the support act's set.

Even if he had wanted to, Blackmore couldn't join his band mates for the jam session as he was hospitalised immediately after the tour to have his appendix removed. This resulted in German and Italian shows scheduled for the end of the month being rearranged for the end of May. But the break from group activity at least gave Jon Lord the chance to record his 'Gemini Suite.' Lord told the press: "Although this will be a strictly Jon Lord production, among the musicians involved will be Roger Glover and Ian Paice as well as Tony Ashton, Albert Lee and Yvonne Elliman. I've asked Keith Emerson to come and play as well, if he has time." While the live performance of the work had been done with Deep Purple, neither Blackmore nor Gillan were remotely interested in being involved in the studio work. The teaming up with Tony Ashton of Ashton, Gardner & Dyke fame was just one of several projects that Lord and Ashton would collaborate on over the ensuing years. Ashton, Gardner & Dyke had been signed to Purple's management company HEC and had a top three single with 'The Resurrection Shuffle' at the beginning of the year. It was also around this time that Tony Edwards came up with the idea for Deep Purple to record the soundtrack for a Western B movie called 'The Last Rebel,' but this was eventually co-written by Jon Lord and Tony Ashton and performed by Ashton, Gardner & Dyke. The pair also started working on another album project, but Lord's commitments to Deep Purple meant that the recording sessions would be sporadic over the next three years.

While the band's primary objective should have been to finish off the new album, by this time only a handful of tracks had been written. Amongst these were a number called 'I'm Alone' and a song about a prostitute called 'Strange Kind Of Woman.' These were coupled together and released in February, with the latter as the a-side. This certainly kept the band in the eye of the rock fraternity while the rest of the album was still being written. 'Strange Kind Of Woman' soon became another top ten hit and helped to stabilise Purple as a major force to be reckoned with. Meanwhile, 'In Rock' was still in the UK charts and Roger Glover spoke to Jackie magazine about its success and what fans could expect to get with the follow-up: "We're still very proud of that album because it showed where we were at that time. It was a stand ... not a collection of bits and pieces and other people's songs, but our music at that point in time. We're still the same band, but we've moved on since then. In the next album we'll be stretching out a bit and the music will have slightly more variation."

At one point during the recording sessions Ian Paice made a startling discovery whilst walking around the studio. Roger Glover documented this at the time: "Ian Paice was walking around carrying his snare drum and hitting it. As he walked from the studio area into the corridor on his way to the control room, he noticed the change in sound of his snare drum. It was so dramatic that he called us all in and demonstrated the difference between the quiet 'toc' of the drum in the soundproofed, padded and baffled studio, and the resounding crash of the drum in the corridor, bringing out the full range of sound ... the real sound, exciting and loud! From that point to the end of the making of 'Fireball', Ian set his drums up in the corridor, greatly inconveniencing everybody, but getting such a good sound that we all forgave him."

Recording sessions continued to be squeezed into the tight schedule as and when, at both De Lane Lea and Olympic studios, just south of the Thames in Barnes. Yet by May even the record companies were getting impatient, particularly in America where the band was scheduled to tour in July and Warner Bros desperately needed a new album to promote on the back of the upcoming tour. Unfortunately the record company would have to wait. May also saw the band's first visit to Australia, where they played five shows in four days and, with travel days included, were actually only away from home for an astonishing eight days. The gigs were all part of an impressive three bill line-up with Free and Manfred Mann's Earth Band, and culminated with a show at Randwick Racecourse in Sydney to an audience of 30,000.

Following a handful of dates scattered around Europe, it was back to England for a couple of one nighters. A couple of weeks of solid studio work were eventually set-aside for early June, yet still they failed to complete the album. Warner Brothers' impatience was wearing thin and they opted to release the album by including the single 'Strange Kind Of Woman.' To pacify impatient British fans awaiting the new album, Ian Gillan promised that when the album would be released, it would include an extended version of the single track. As it was, the US version of the album released in July actually included a slightly longer take than had been released on the single, with a lengthier guitar fade out. The album was finally completed in June when 'Demon's Eye' was laid down.

Purple's popularity in America was still going through a rebuilding process, and following a few smaller headlining gigs in early July they spent the rest of the month touring the States second on the bill to The Faces. Given the treatment dished out by Blackmore some years earlier to Faces vocalist Rod Stewart, it is unfortunate that there are no sources telling how Blackmore felt having to be part of the support act. At one of the gigs Rod Stewart invited the audience back to the hotel, although it was Deep Purple's hotel that he elected to announce on stage, and Roger Glover recalled, "it was absolute chaos. 3,000 kids in the lobby, up the elevators and on the stairs." Was this Stewart's way of repaying Blackmore? If so it was undoubtedly a harmless prank and it is unlikely that there was much in the way of bitterness between them. Indeed there were occasions on the tour when the pair teamed up for a spot of mayhem. In Minneapolis, Warner Brothers hosted a joint party for the two bands and Blackmore and Stewart started a food fight that ended up in total chaos, with Warner's representative Russ Shaw being dumped into a laundry bag and unceremoniously thrown in to the swimming pool! When the hotel manager intervened, Blackmore wrapped a fire hose around him until he looked like the Michelin Man. The damage was reported to have been $25,000, for which the unfortunate record company picked up the tab.

Away from the off stage mayhem, on stage Purple was going down a storm and eyewitnesses reported that at several shows they were received with much greater enthusiasm than the headliners. The tour went a long way to re-establishing Purple in the most lucrative of markets, as well as introducing Purple to a new audience of fans. For some of these new fans such as Mike Hill, the experience of seeing Deep Purple was truly staggering. Hill saw the show at the Long Beach Arena in California and waxed lyrical about it in a wonderfully vivid manner. Following the opening act Matthew's Southern Comfort, Deep Purple took to the stage, as Hill's takes up the story: "The first group came out and played and then it was time for Deep Purple. Everywhere the lights were killed. An invisible, dark power emanating from the stage was exerting a hush upon us. It was the bass player, organist and drummer forcing our ears into submission. They seemed to be tuning up, testing, testing. Scary, almost creepy it was, to hear and feel that intensity, yet not be able to see it. When the organ, bass and drums could ascend no higher in

decibels the lead guitar came winging into this intimidating warm-up of a prelude, with monstrous screeches as turquoise spotlights played over the stage.

"All the instruments poured into a catchy beat and the lead singer kicked the tempo up a notch higher by singing that he was a 'Speed King.' Bright white mini floodlights centred on the singer and guitarist as other red and navy blue lights funnelled in figure-of-eight arcs everywhere else on the stage. They were all playing extremely fast, very loud and the rhythm couldn't be beat. This opening song featured a note for note duel between the singer and guitarist. The guitar would perfectly duplicate the squeals of the vocalist, and quite amazingly, vice versa. Neither performer could top the other, so they both exploded out of the contest, the singer delivering supersonic, space bending peals of laughter into the mic and the guitarist wrapping the guitar completely around his body and bringing it to rest facing him at a 45 degree angle to his chest. In a recess between the organ and drums stood the bassist, whilst I caught glimpses of a blur of hair, elbows and sticks that was the drummer. The performers swung back into the "I'm a Speed King! You gotta hear me sing" refrain, with the drummer pushing it even faster. This band was unquestionably hot, unique and the way they played this classic rock song with such gusto had me thinking it was the most memorable number I'd heard since Elvis' Jailhouse Rock. It brought back that kind of excitement I had as a kid. Brilliance came easy to this group.

"The next song was an instrumental that I later learned was called 'Wring That Neck.' That guitarist really asserted himself on the stage with a grandiose mien and clearly set the tempo. They played in perfect unity for at least ten minutes until the guitarist decided it was time for a break. He backed out of his spotlight, mopped his face with a towel and vanished behind his amps. The organist played rock, classical and even baroque music. More people would attend church if the choir's pipes could be reamed the way this guy did it. The music was of such an inviting beauty that it soon discovered the deepest chambers of the heart. It was rich by any Hammond's standards. Then the bass and guitar synthesised to bring the instrumental around to the opening bars.

What happened from there was truly shocking. The guitarist stepped forward and began to thrash the guitar's neck with his left hand. Both the plectrum hand and the other buzzed so rapidly over the instrument that I couldn't believe my eyes. He stood there picking almost every rhythm and melody imaginable. Each string and every fret got worked over, up and down in an ecstasy of guitar virtuosity. He was proving to us that he could play loud and fast rock, western, and even classical too. This was a long instrumental, as for at least twenty minutes the band had been displaying its expertise on this number. Faster, louder, teeters, and then in a split second he quit playing and the spotlight expired on the guitar finial. We thrilled fans applauded and shouted to the darkened stage. Then the spotlight clicked back on stage left and the guitarist stepped back into it and played some very pretty Elizabethan music, whilst 'Greensleeves' was interpolated next. Incredibly 'Jingle Bells' was next on the bill of fare, before the band lustily poured in again. He moved to the edge of the stage and folded to his knees whilst playing faster and faster to the end of the song.

"The next song started off sombrely with the organ. The singer mourned about a 'Child In Time.' Beautifully he wailed on at times sounding like an adolescent girl in tears. Near the end of his crying his troubled soul expressed itself in one long, momentously bittersweet scream. The singer split, leaving these noteworthy performers to carry on the sublime way he began. All the instruments rocked away and each musician forced it to the limits. It became evident then and there that this mysterious thin man in black was rocking-out, not only with the guitar in the most unlikely positions, but in impossible ways no one had ever dreamed of before, not even Hendrix. The guitarist executed an outlandishly nimble refrain and the number was over, or so we thought. We all applauded uproariously, but the band didn't leave. Soon the crooner was out there again screaming sobs into the mic, before he released some screamed yells, a colossal harp was plucked from nowhere and the magnificent song concluded.

They didn't waste much time getting into the next one, which had perhaps the most infectious beat of them all. The vocalist started singing something about a 'Mandrake Root,' which was 'screaming in his braaain!' The singer split and the song settled into an instrumental. The organist did his thing, making the keys creak, spin and sputter. He teased us with unexpected snatches of Dvorak's 'New World Symphony,' the music soaring ahead of, and out of, the tracks the other three laid down. When he felt we'd had enough of the serenade he began swiping at the keys, making the machine snarl. He got up off his seat and kneeled on the throttled keys further, a showman himself.

"The guitarist now emerged from the wings, then un-strapped the guitar and threw it down. Thereupon, he stood on it, actually playing music, not feedback. From our seats it appeared he was fretting with one foot and somehow picking with the other. Picking the guitar up, he proceeded to play what I can only describe as flute-like music. He then unloaded a flurry of notes that sounded like a machine-gun, which taunted the organist who repeated the notes in kind. We were put through a thorough workout, beholding his guitar gymnastics. This potent Mandrake Root stuff was the greatest demonstration of creative energy output I'd ever experienced. He approached the mic stand and sawed the guitar back and forth on the shaft and then tied it to the stand with his shoulder strap, before slapping the machine head so that it began to spin. He left the stage and the house lights came up on an abandoned stage, the rest of the band having left during all of this. An announcer walked on, and over our grateful adulation shouted, "From England! Deep Purple!" All about me people lauded the set; it was not only the greatest group I'd ever seen, it was the greatest entertainment ever for me. I sat winded; my senses had been pulverised."

When 'Fireball' finally saw the light of day in Europe in September, exactly a year after it had been started, Ian Gillan's promise of an extended version of 'Strange Kind Of Woman' never materialised. The last track they had recorded wasn't wasted and 'Demon's Eye' was included instead of the hit single. As such, America (and Japan) were the only countries to release the album with 'Strange Kind Of Woman.' If chart places are anything to go by then 'Fireball' was definitely a success. The band had built up a huge following since the release of 'In Rock' and from the great concert reviews throughout the press. 'Fireball' thus soon reached number one in Britain, yet the album wasn't given the thumbs up in quite the same way that 'In Rock' had been. Perhaps mindful of the time that dragged from start to finish, even the band seemed less than enamoured with it. Blackmore particularly seemed disappointed with the results: "There are only three tracks that I think are good – 'No No No,' 'Fools' & 'Fireball' itself," he was quoted as saying shortly after its release. The others were less damning but remained sceptical of it. The exception to the rule was Ian Gillan, who to this day cites it as his favourite album.

After the full-on assault of 'In Rock,' 'Fireball' was probably something of a surprise to many listeners who may have been expecting something similar to the previous release. Sure the opening title track, also released as a single, was an out an out belter, but the album showed another side to Deep Purple's music. In the days when it was hip to be 'progressive,' Fireball fully embodied that ethic and this is perhaps another reason why the album tends to be overlooked today. Reviews in the press were something of a mixed bag. One reviewer wrote, "'Fireball' is undiluted funky Purple. The songs all seem rather bitter-sweet but create good feelings all the same." However, another simply stated that the album "surpasses anything Deep Purple has so far produced on record."

Due to its greater diversity of styles and sound, 'Fireball' had the tendency to confuse some listeners. Tracks such as 'No No No' and 'Fools' showed a more imaginative side to the band; 'Demon's Eye' was a clever blues romp unlike anything the band had done before, whereas 'The Mule' proved to be very off the wall. The lyrics for this were along way from traditional rock 'n' roll fare, having been inspired by a sci-fi novel, with suitable spacey music – perhaps more in the mould of Hawkwind or Pink Floyd than Deep Purple. The most unusual number of all was probably the last track on side one, 'Anyone's Daughter.' This must have tested the fans more than anything. It is pure country, with an almost Bob Dylan-style talkin' blues vocal line. Suitably countrified piano and guitar solos round off the number. The closing cut on the LP, 'No One Came,' was a perfect example of 'progressive rock.' Although a powerful pounding piece of music, both Gillan's tongue in cheek lyrics and the clever arrangement of the music showed that Purple was more than just a 'heavy' band.

It has been well documented that the unusual opening to the title track is the sound of the studio's air-conditioning unit being turned on, but less well documented is the story behind this. Mike Thorne was the assistant to engineer Martin Birch and recalls, "come Christmas Eve 1970, I was that tea boy, still bright-eyed and bushy-tailed, eager for action and to learn something new. Since it was the holiday season, no one had booked the studio, so I was restricted to hanging out in the cramped reception area of De Lane Lea Music, chatting with receptionist Andrea. That studio, like many spaces which have nurtured great work, was without music, really just an uninspiring and shabby basement. I was terminally bored, with no agenda save waiting for the boss's phone call to permit us to start our holidays. Boredom has its cures, and the studio air-conditioning was to be my artistic and technical focus until the releasing phone call. I had enjoyed the singular sound that the air-conditioning made in the string section microphones when it was turned on after a take. Yet it came to be that this air conditioning unit was perhaps the most appreciated in recording history, even though the fans didn't know. It was my first hit recording (sort of)."

Thorne took it upon himself to get the sound down on tape: "Several massively expensive tube mics were placed strategically in the grubby air conditioning closet. With a little plate reverb, not to mention fastidious mic placing refined by control room checks, I created what to my beginner's ears was a most enveloping stereo machine sound. I turned the machine on, waited a little after it had climaxed to appreciate the full roar, then turned it off. I faded the recording, edited out the click with a razor blade, and put the master in a box with credit to the singular performance of the 'West Uzbekistan Percussion Ensemble.' It was just after the sixties had closed, so please humour me. The master went into the tape store, where it languished forgotten until an innovative client request."

After 'Fireball' had been recorded, an idea was suggested to Birch, as Thorne explains: "one of the group, probably Roger Glover, turned to Martin and said, 'what we need to get this track (and the album) going is the sound of a machine starting up.'" He continues: "'The West Uzbekistan Percussion Ensemble' masterpiece was immediately grafted, to be the start of the opening track, although it had to be transferred in mono for the mix since my glorious stereo could not pass through the limitations of a 16-channel mixing desk and an eight-track multi-track tape recorder. A happy session concluded with delighted clients. I forgot about my tape, happy that I'd contributed my first widely heard sounds, in the enforced rush of carrying out my final clear-your-desk marching orders."

Shortly after the release of 'Fireball,' with the band's success ever-increasing, the management established its own label, something that was fast becoming a common practice with top acts: The Beatles, The Rolling Stones and Moody Blues had all established their own labels, and in October '71 Purple Records was launched. The company's advertising slogan was, 'The Open Ear,' and the label would prove to be an outlet for individual members' solo and production work, as well as being a home for an array of eclectic talent. Artists signed to the label included Bullet, a three-piece band consisting of ex-Atomic Rooster's John Du Cann and Paul Hammond, and Quatermass's John Gustafson (they soon changed the name to Hard Stuff). Other acts included Hawaiian vocalist Yvonne Elliman and Glam rockers Silverhead, who featured lead singer Michael Des Barres and future Blondie bassist, Nigel Harrison. The label even released a single by Dr Who actor Jon Pertwee called 'Who Is The Doctor?' It has to be said that, apart from Deep Purple itself, virtually none of the label's releases by the other acts were particularly successful, although some of the artists did go on to establish successful careers outside of the Purple Records confines. Amongst the first batch of releases on Purple Records was the re-recorded, re-arranged studio recording of Jon Lord's 'Gemini Suite.'

A wonderful side story worth mentioning is that Purple Records also signed a duo called Curtiss Maldoon. This was born out of Bodast, a group that had featured none other than Bobby Woodman and Dave Curtiss after their departure from the embryonic Deep Purple, as well as guitarist Steve Howe who went on to greater things with Yes. Bodast had also been signed by HEC after Woodman and Curtiss had approached Purple's management. As Woodman recalls, "even though they sacked us we went back a year later when we had put this band together and said to John Coletta, 'we have a great new band would you be interested in signing us?' and we recorded an album." Unfortunately the record wasn't released at the time and the recordings didn't see the light of day until 1981. Bodast was a short-lived band that split up in December '69; however, Bodast was around long enough for Woodman to have one further encounter with Blackmore, who was in attendance at one of the band's gigs at London's Speakeasy club in June '69. Woodman recently informed the author that Blackmore approached Curtiss himself and asked if he could get up and jam with them. Seeing there was opportunity to try and get one over on the man who was part responsible for ousting him from Purple, Woodman said "if you can find some musicians to play with, because you're not playing with us – you can fuck off you wanker," after which the band promptly left the stage and retired to the bar!

Following the successful American tour, and with 'Fireball' now released, the band embarked on a full scale British tour, as opposed to the one nighters they had been doing. But if fans were expecting to hear many of the songs from the new album, they were disappointed. As evidence of the group's general lack of enthusiasm for the album, little of the material became established as regular concert numbers. 'Strange Kind Of Woman' had been brought into the stage set earlier in the year and soon became a firm stage favourite, but of course, at least as far as Europe was concerned, this wasn't strictly a 'Fireball' track. Ironically, 'Demon's Eye,' the track left off the US version of the album, was played during the July American tour but was soon dropped from the set. 'No One Came' had been tried out at the Camden Arts Festival back in

April, but as it was still unreleased at the time, the audience was unfamiliar with it and it wasn't played again. The same fate met 'Anyone's Daughter.' Having been played a few times during UK dates in June, it was axed. 'No No No' was also briefly played, including a live performance on German TV's The Beat Club, shortly before the album's European release. 'Fireball' itself was occasionally performed live as an encore, but as a hell for leather number the band tended more often than not to stick with their interpretation of Little Richard's 'Lucille' as a more suitable end of show song. 'The Mule' turned out to be the only track that became an integral part of the stage act, albeit in a greatly revamped way as it was used as a showcase for Ian Paice's drum solo, replacing 'Paint It Black' in the process. The only other piece from the album that found its way into the live set on a regular basis was the slow middle section of 'Fools,' with Blackmore using his volume control technique to produce what was often described as his "cello effect." In fact this instrumental passage had already been frequently used on stage during the long instrumental section of 'Mandrake Root.'

As the UK tour kicked off at the Guildhall, Portsmouth, new material was already being developed. In fact while travelling on the bus to that first gig, legend has it that Blackmore came up with a new riff. The band had been scratching around for a fast, driving number to replace 'Speed King' as the set opener and, after working on the idea at the sound check, Gillan added some impromptu lyrics and the song opened the show that night. The band themselves have relayed this story, but other sources claim that the song was already written and that Blackmore didn't actually travel with the band to this gig as he was keen to avoid the journalists, an attitude that continues in his career today. Although it has yet to be clarified one way or the other, the most important thing was the song itself: 'Highway Star.' Further evidence that the band was not happy with 'Fireball' was the inclusion of another new track added for the tour. 'Lazy,' a bluesy shuffle, had been written during tour rehearsals and was brought into the set, initially as a set closer to replace 'Mandrake Root,' but by now 'Wring That Neck' had also finally been put to bed after three years in the set. The support act for the tour were new Purple Record's signing Bullet, and the tour included a return to the Royal Albert Hall, although of course there was no orchestra to be seen!

Although this terminology wasn't used at the time, this second Deep Purple line-up would eventually become known as MKII. Apparently, referring to the different line-ups in this way originally resulted from the band's accountants, in order to make it easier to distinguish between them for the purpose of royalties. Meanwhile, even though the amount of money now rolling in was increasing at a much greater rate, so too was the friction within the band. Chiefly this was between Ian Gillan and Ritchie Blackmore. There can be no denying that both men were largely instrumental in helping the group's rapid rise to fame and fortune, but equally neither of them could accept anything less than 'top-dog' status. Since the "Concerto," Blackmore had taken up the reigns as the group's principal composer and major driving force, but following his success as 'Jesus Christ Superstar,' Ian Gillan was certainly a major focal point with the audience. Even though Blackmore was the riffmeister, without Gillan's soaring voice Blackmore's vision for a harder sound would not have been fulfilled, and both men clearly saw their roles as the most important within the band. The inevitable egos grew as rapidly as their record sales and it appeared that no one had the vision or maturity to deal with it.

Capitalising on the successful summer tour of America supporting The Faces, another month of touring kicked off on 22nd October at New York City's Felt Forum. However, what should have pushed Purple's stature in America back to the levels of 1968 was sadly curtailed when Ian Gillan took ill in Chicago after just two shows. Gillan was admitted to hospital with hepatitis and, although the gig that evening went ahead with Roger Glover doing all the vocals, it was apparent that, as tuneful as Glover's singing may have been, he was no replacement for Gillan's huge voice and the rest of the tour was cancelled. Although in later years Glover commented that it was nice to say he had once sung lead vocals for the band, he also added that he was glad the show wasn't bootlegged, at least as far as is known, as no recording of the show has ever surfaced.

If relationships between Ian Gillan and Ritchie Blackmore had soured, at least the break gave the pair an opportunity for some breathing space. But while Gillan recuperated at home, Blackmore took the opportunity of a busman's holiday and briefly returned to the studio. As well as the ego clashes, Blackmore was also becoming disillusioned with Gillan's singing style, and had visions of a more bluesy approach, something that he claimed the singer had absolutely no interest in. Blackmore had visions of a Jimi Hendrix Experience type band, and a young, half-

Irish, black bassist-cum-vocalist named Phil Lynott had caught Blackmore's eye earlier in the year. Lynott was the front man for Irish trio Thin Lizzy who had moved to London earlier in the year to further their career. The self-titled debut album was released in April and Blackmore, along with Ian Paice, spent a couple of days jamming and recording with Lynott. The project was referred to as 'Baby Face,' but the tapes were nothing more than rough jams, according to those who have heard them.

By early December Ian Gillan had recuperated from his illness and the press was informed that the band was travelling to Switzerland to record the next album. Such was Purple's growing success that they were advised by HEC's accountant Bill Reid to record abroad and benefit from the resulting tax advantages. 'Fireball' would prove to be the last album that Deep Purple would record in England. Even though Blackmore and Paice had one eye on their 'Baby Face' project, the month break had regenerated the batteries of the entire band. Blackmore was looking forward to making the next album, tentatively titled 'Machine Head.' "This next album will show people what Purple's future really is. I personally didn't like the last one," he told the press, "but I think this one will really get to the people."

'Fireball' may not have been a favourite with the band, but Paice's startling discovery regarding the drum sound had inspired Purple to go the full hog with the next album and get away from the studio entirely. Switzerland had not only been picked for tax reasons, but the Casino in Montreux was a regular venue on the touring circuit and they saw it as the perfect place to record an album under live performance conditions, minus the audience of course. The venue acoustics would be perfect for producing a far more natural sound than the stifled acoustics of a padded and baffled studio. That said, as they were not going to record in a conventional studio, the album would not have been possible without the Rolling Stones Mobile Unit. The Stones mobile unit was the first of its kind in the world. Originally decked out with an 8-track recording facility, it was soon upgraded to 16-track and from the outside it resembled an army truck with its camouflaged green paint job. It was a widely used facility and Led Zeppelin had recorded its third and fourth albums with the mobile. Along with hiring the truck came the Stones own crewmembers Jeremy Gee and Nick Watterton. The mobile's manager Ian Stewart also went along to Montreux for the first few days to ensure that everything was working fine. They also took their own regular engineer Martin Birch. Birch had worked on Deep Purple's albums since 'The Book Of Taliesyn' when he was the assistant to Barry Ainsworth, the engineer at London's De Lane Lea Studios. By the time that 'In Rock' was recorded, Birch had become De Lane Lea's chief engineer, but as both 'In Rock' and 'Fireball' were recorded at more than one studio, Birch had only been involved in some of the tracks, although the band was quick to recognise his talents. Birch had engineered the track 'Hard Lovin' Man' from 'In Rock,' and as a consequence was credited on the album as a catalyst.

Glover in particular took a lot of interest in the recording aspects of the band and said, "the chemistry between the band and Martin was instant. He felt like one of us." Ian Paice concurred, "Martin Birch was a great engineer. For his time he was streets ahead of anybody in England." Birch had also worked with Fleetwood Mac, engineering the 1969 album 'Then Play On.' He later went on to produce Fleetwood Mac shortly after the sojourn in Montreux. In what has now become one of the most documented stories in rock folklore, events unfolded that severely hampered the band's plans. On arrival, Claude Nobs, the venue's promoter and organiser, invited the band to the final concert to be held in the Casino prior to the winter shutdown, after which the plan was for the band to take up residency there to record the album. The concert by Frank

Zappa and the Mothers turned into a disaster when, midway through it, someone in the audience fired a flare gun into the wooden roof. In next to no time, the entire building had been evacuated and subsequently burnt to the ground. Fortunately everyone managed to get out unscathed, but Zappa lost all his equipment and Purple lost their recording venue.

Deep Purple had actually gone to Montreux to appear at the Casino, and they planned to record an album there under simulated live concert conditions and then to cut another in 'studio' one of new songs and issue them as a double package. But the fire put a stop to all of this. "Trying to find somewhere to record wasn't easy," said Purple's co-manager, John Coletta. Despite all the problems on his hands, after a couple of days Claude Nobs had found the band a new venue. 'Le Pavilion' was an old concert hall also not in use at the time and seemed ideal. As soon as the band moved into 'Le Pavilion' they started working on a new riff idea that Blackmore had come up with. It was after midnight before they were happy with the arrangement and started recording a few takes. Unfortunately the locals didn't take kindly to being kept awake by the excessive volume Deep Purple was making. Unbeknown to the band, the roadies had been holding the doors shut to prevent the police from entering and stopping them from working. Fortunately they got a finished take they were happy with before the police finally put a stop to the evening's work. As was often the case with the way Purple worked, the backing track was given a 'working' title before Gillan had written lyrics for it, but at least 'Title No.1,' as it was temporarily called, was completed.

Because the band preferred to work at night, their second recording venue was now also out of bounds. Several days went by with them sitting around doing nothing as Claude Nobs searched desperately for another venue. Eventually they managed to take over the ground floor area of the Grand Hotel,

another building closed for the season. The main attraction of this building was that it still retained the lack of padding and soundproofing, which enabled the sounds of the instruments to crash around the walls of the vast building. In the intervening days, Roger Glover recalled waking up one morning having dreamt about the fire and said to himself out loud, "smoke on the water." Initially he thought nothing more of it, but it would form the basis of the lyrics that Ian Gillan would write to document the experiences they had just gone through. The lyrics were used for 'Title No.1' and Deep Purple's most famous song was completed. Although they had lost around a week with the disruptions, by mid winter's day eight tracks had been completed. As 'Highway Star' and 'Lazy' had been written before the UK tour, in effect only six new tracks had been composed during their stay in Montreux. "We got kicked out of two places we tried because of the noise but eventually we found the Grand Hotel which has been closed for redecoration," explained John Coletta at the time.

A few days after the fire, Roger Glover explained to the press that the Casino, which was insured for £1,400,000, would take up to two years to re-build. He also gave an eyewitness account explaining what happened: "a gentleman of Oriental or Asiatic origin let off a distress flare which ignited the ceiling and soon the whole place was engulfed in flames. I was watching the band and everyone started turning round looking towards the back, so I turned round to see what was happening and I heard a crackling sound which was the roof burning. I thought it had gone out and I hung around for about seven minutes; then wandered aimlessly outside because everyone else was. A few minutes later the whole place went up."

In between the sessions, the band also managed to find time to fly back to England for an appearance on 'Top Of The Pops,' performing 'Fireball' which had been released as a single a few weeks earlier. During the making of the album Ian Gillan expressed how happy he was with proceedings: "This one has been done very quickly and the main reason it's going so well is that we had a month off before we did it and we were all keyed up and eager to do it. We've been here just over a week but we took three days off to fly back to England to do 'Top Of The Pops' and we've still almost finished it. There are two more backing tracks to lay down tonight and tomorrow and I've got a couple more songs to do then we're finished, it'll take about ten days in all." Glover concurred, "This is the best album we've ever done, by far the best. The atmosphere has been really great." Maybe because of the upheavals involved, the guys knuckled down with the work and the album was recorded in a far more congenial atmosphere than one could have expected a few months earlier.

Although 'Machine Head' would not be released for several months, 1972 started well for the band with what would be the first of many American tours that took them through to an end date in Idaho on 31st January. However, both Blackmore and Gillan's behaviour on the road started to bring an air of chaos to the band, with ever-increasing displays of petulance, disruption and conflict. They appeared to delight in causing trouble and applying the Joan Collins philosophy that "no publicity is bad publicity." They clearly saw that the big stirs they would often make got them free publicity in the next day's paper. Although some of the antics were nothing more than pranks, others sometimes took on a more sinister tone. As far as sound engineer Bob Simon's experiences were concerned, it was Ian Gillan who was the first to set the ball rolling with his unruly behaviour. At a gig in Detroit Ian Gillan discovered that a couple of the road crew had been given a hard time by the local union officials and sought his revenge: "During the show Ian walked over to me in the middle of the song and said, 'how much do you want to bet me I can bust that microphone stand all over this stage?' I looked at him and said, 'I'll bet you a couple of bucks you can't.' He walked back out there and took the microphone stand and started digging big holes in that rubber flooring. Those union guys flipped out. We got Ian in the limo straight after the show and got him out of there. Gillan was the first with that kind of action that I saw and then as Gillan kind of faded away Ritchie took over and intentionally didn't turn up for shows. We had five major riots with those guys I went through for not showing up."

February and March were set-aside for sporadic gigs throughout Europe, including a concert at the BBC's Paris Theatre studio for broadcast on Radio 1. It gave fans the chance to hear the new songs well in advance of the album's release and no fewer than six of the new songs were performed. Mid March saw the band back in America, but as with the tour at the end of the previous year it didn't go quite as planned. Just a couple of weeks into the tour Blackmore succumbed to the same illness that had inflicted Ian Gillan, and on 31st March at a gig in Flint, Michigan the band had to perform as a four piece once again while Blackmore was hospitalised with hepatitis. It was another terrible set back, coming at a time when Purple were re-establishing themselves in America and, although the next few shows were instantly cancelled, they seriously considered trying to carry on with a replacement.

With the potential earnings to be gained from the tour, the pressure was on to continue. Blackmore's guitar was undeniably a huge focal point for Deep Purple, but if a suitable replacement could be found, it was possible the tour could be completed. At least that was the thinking within the camp and legendary session player Al Kooper was the first guy they approached. Kooper was an unusual choice because, despite his talent, he was most well known as a keyboard player as a result of his work with Bob Dylan on classic tracks such as 'Positively Fourth Street' and 'Like A Rolling Stone.'

Kooper had just completed a tour with his band Blood, Sweat And Tears, which ironically saw him also end up in hospital. He had only been out for three weeks when his agent who was handling the Purple tour called him. He pleaded with Kooper to help both himself and Purple out of a situation that was otherwise potentially going to end in financial disaster with the cancellation of further shows. Kooper was invited to audition the following day: "I was dumbfounded. First of all, I was a keyboard player, a fair one at that, who dabbled on guitar," he recalled many years later. "Ritchie Blackmore was a master of the genre he participated in – light years from where I would ever end up. Secondly, I barely knew any of their songs and most of all, I had just finished a tour that had put me in the hospital."

Somewhat reluctantly, armed with his Epiphone Wilshire guitar Kooper went through his audition. Knowing some of the band from the touring circuit certainly helped matters. "They started playing something pretty simple," he explained, "and I joined in." However, Kooper recalls that the next number they tried out "was really fast." It would most certainly have been either 'Highway Star' or 'Child In Time,' and Kooper admitted, "It was simply too fast for me to play a solo."

The rest of Deep Purple weren't put off, and any parts that Kooper wasn't up to Jon Lord could comfortably cover on organ. As the audition concluded Purple and the road crew were delighted with Kooper's handling of the situation and agreed that he was the man for the job. Kooper felt otherwise and it didn't take him long on his journey home to decide that he just wasn't up for it. He clearly didn't want to let anyone down, but filling Ritchie Blackmore's shoes was way beyond Kooper's abilities with a six-string. He broke the decision to his distraught agent over the phone. The least that Kooper felt obliged to do was to suggest an alternative guitarist, namely one of his personal favourites, Randy California. California was well known for his work with the West Coast outfit Spirit that he had left the previous year in order to pursue a solo career.

Born Randy Wolfe in Los Angeles on 20th February 1951. The stage name 'Randy California' was given to Wolfe by Jimi Hendrix, with whom he played in New York in 1966, and this was done in order to distinguish him from another Randy in the band. After a couple of days rehearsing at New York's Fillmore East Deep, Purple continued the tour on 6th April in Quebec City, Canada with Randy California deputising for the hospitalised Blackmore. Perhaps given the bitter feelings that had developed, and would continue to do so, between Ian Gillan and Ritchie Blackmore, the show was very enjoyable for the singer and he also recalled that the band was well received. Gillan was impressed with California's performance and most notably with the guitarist's decision to play the solo in 'Child In Time' on slide guitar. The other most memorable thing about the show was the inclusion of 'When A Blind Man Cries.' This delightful if not uncharacteristic blues gem in the Purple catalogue was recorded for the 'Machine Head' album, but bizarrely Blackmore didn't like it and it wasn't included on the album. Instead it sneaked out as the B-side to the single 'Never Before' that was released a month or so after this gig. It was to be the only time Deep Purple played the number on stage during the 1970s.

Despite enjoying the experience, Purple realised how crucial Blackmore's contribution was to the band. Although they dearly would have loved to see the tour completed, the remaining dates were reluctantly cancelled. Ironically it was Ian Gillan who years later publicly defended the decision: "I don't think it would have been right to carry on without Ritchie. They didn't carry on without me when I was ill and that had a lot to do with the decision to cancel." The knock on effect was potentially damaging to the band's growing success. Cancelling the tour meant that, in turn, three concerts planned for the band's first visit to Japan in mid May were also cancelled and rescheduled for August. On their return to Britain, Blackmore had to spend time convalescing in a nursing home and Jon Lord talked to the press about the misfortunes that were dogging the band: "I'm trying to work out what we've done wrong. It doesn't seem fair that the same group gets hit twice by hepatitis in six months – both times in the middle of an American tour. It seems that every time we go there we take two steps forward and one step back."

- CHAPTER FOUR -
HIGHWAY STARS

THE CANCELLATION of an American tour for a second time might well have been a setback for the band. However, as fate would have it, the spare time that resulted from Blackmore's illness led to important twists in many people's careers. Bruce Payne, Deep Purple's then booking agent, had set up an audition with Columbia Records in New York for a small-time outfit that he was managing called Elf. Payne took Paice and Glover along to the audition and they were so impressed that they offered to produce the band's debut album. Elf's keyboard player Mickey Lee Soule recalled the events in an interview three years ago: "Our manager worked for a major booking agency in New York and had gotten us an audition with Columbia Records. Deep Purple was about to start a tour of the U.S when Ritchie came down with hepatitis and had to cancel the tour. By chance, Roger and Ian Paice were hanging around the agency office just as we arrived. We met them and they decided to tag along to the rehearsal hall where we were to audition. The dudes from Columbia (Clive Davis was one) sat in folding chairs in front of us smoking cigars. You could tell by looking at them that they didn't have a clue about the music. Very difficult scene for us under normal circumstances, but the Columbia boys knew who Deep Purple were. Luckily, Roger and Paicey were knocked out, and I'm sure this made the decision easier for Clive and the boys. We were offered a deal, and with sudden time on their hands, Roger and Ian offered to produce. Within days we were in Atlanta recording." This rather unexpected

collaboration was the start of a long association between Elf and Deep Purple. For Elf's lead singer, Ronnie James Dio, his relationship with Blackmore, the one member of Deep Purple who was back in Britain at the time of this initial get together, would prove to be the most fruitful. Elf soon became the regular support act for Purple, initially just in the States, but eventually throughout Europe as well.

By the time that Blackmore had recovered from his bout of hepatitis 'Machine Head' had been released and, like 'Fireball,' it reached number one in the UK charts. However, the album was also a massive success in America and within a few months the album track 'Smoke On The Water' was getting a huge amount of airplay on FM radio stations across the States. The rest of '72 would see Purple focus on a full-scale assault of America, with four further extensive tours throughout Canada and the USA. While it was a time of huge financial success for the band, bitterness and intolerance within the group continued to grow at alarming rates.

There was just time between American tours to slot in two dates at London's Rainbow Theatre on 30th June and 1st July. These shows launched the re-opening of the venue, but the band only agreed to do them if the orchestra pit were filled in so that there would be closer contact with the audience. As the brace of gigs looked likely to be the only ones in the UK for the foreseeable future, the keenest fans queued outside the venue overnight, and when the box office opened in the morning it was estimated that more then 1,000 people were outside. Younger fans reading this should note that, in the days before the Internet or even credit card bookings over the telephone, there were only two ways to get tickets for gigs: either send off a cheque in the post, or queue up at the box office. Furthermore the gigs landed Purple with the title of 'loudest band in the world' when the local authority recorded the volume at 117 decibels. Whether or not Deep Purple was actually the loudest band in the world is certainly open to question. It wasn't common practice to monitor decibel levels, so it was certainly feasible that other bands were emitting even more decibels. The Who's gig at Charlton Football Ground three years later was also monitored and exceeded Purple's volume, soon losing Purple its notoriety, although this title continued to be used to describe the band. As sound systems have become more substantial and sophisticated, numerous groups regularly exceed the decibel levels set at this concert.

In between the third and fourth US tours, the band took time out to work on the next album, with three weeks earmarked in Italy to lay the tracks down. Having produce a trilogy of studio albums that represented the finest hard rock of its era, the expectations that Deep Purple would produce another album of equal quality was all too obvious. Less apparent at the time was the disharmony within the ranks, and by the time MKII came to produce its fourth studio album, there was enormous friction within the band. The now infamous rift between Blackmore and Gillan is well known, but back in the days when Deep Purple was riding on the crest of a wave, the management had always done its best to keep the internal bickering from the public glare.

The arguing that had started around the time of 'Fireball' had been pretty absent during the making of 'Machine Head' when the band had knuckled down on the recordings, but the friction was never far from the surface. The success that had come Deep Purple's way as a direct result of the incredible albums and stage performances would also prove to play a part in the band's demise. The incessant touring and the exhaustion felt within the band were only one negative aspect affecting the group. But Ritchie Blackmore's ever-growing disillusionment with Ian Gillan's vocal style had already sown a seed the previous year in the recordings done with Ian Paice and Phil Lynott. The fact that Blackmore had also considered Free's Paul Rodgers as the vocalist for this project goes some way to explain why his feelings towards Ian Gillan's singing style had changed. Blackmore was, and remains to this day, a huge admirer of Paul Rodgers, and very few would disagree that Rodgers is one of the finest blues-rock vocalists that Britain has ever produced.

From the other side of the fence, Ian Gillan thought that Deep Purple was stagnating and he wanted the band to return to the more progressive approach adopted with 'Fireball,' believing the music was now being produced to a formula. The time isn't fondly remembered by anyone in the band. Although the surroundings were a delightful villa just outside of Rome, Deep Purple treated the time there more as an opportunity to re-charge the batteries and have a well-earned rest. As Roger Glover recalled when working on the remastered release in 1999, "the first order of business was to get a good supply of cheap local wine; hundreds of bottles arrived on the back of a truck." Although the main frictions were between Gillan and Blackmore, who hardly even crossed paths during the three weeks in Italy, Blackmore generally kept himself away from the band and even chose to live in separate accommodation. "The three weeks went by with precious little in the way of progress," according to Glover. "Much of the time was spent waiting for various band members to show up." Only two tracks were completed during the three weeks.

'Painted Horse' was one of those two tracks, and it was also a perfect example of the divisions that had now developed within Deep Purple. Although the band was happy with the backings, once Blackmore had heard Gillan's vocals he took an instant dislike to it. Ian Gillan refused to alter a note, and consequently Ritchie Blackmore stated that he would not allow it to form part of the album. Ian Gillan actually remembers that only Martin Birch supported his belief that the vocal track was

okay. The second track they managed to finish proved to have a better vibe to it. 'Woman From Tokyo' would also become the opening number on the album and lyrically it was inspired by the group's forthcoming trip to Japan. Ian Paice calculated that, as a result of producing only one song for the album during their three weeks in Italy, 'Woman From Tokyo' cost around £8,000.

Box office takings for the next batch of gigs in Japan would soon recoup that cost, and when the band arrived in 'the land of the rising sun' for its first Japanese tour, they were greeted by hordes of fans at Tokyo airport. In reality, to call it a tour is stretching things a bit; the band played just three gigs in two cities: two nights at the Koseinenkin in Osaka, followed by one gig at the world famous Budokan in Tokyo. Deep Purple had always been popular in the Far East, although it's fair to say that the Japanese generally welcomed Western rock music with open arms. The success of the 'Machine Head' album resulted in an extensive period of touring in support of it, but it wasn't until Japan that the idea of a live album came back onto the agenda.

Given Purple's reputation as a live act, it seems strange that it took so long to make an official live recording, and this would probably never have happened without the initial suggestion of Warner Brothers, the Japanese record company who wanted a souvenir of the band's first Japanese tour. Warner's decision to record all three shows would soon prove to be something of a masterstroke. Although plenty of radio and TV work had previously been undertaken, recording live performances for general release was something the band had shied away from up to this point. Deep Purple had paid little attention to recording live albums. Live concerts were always a special experience, and with every show the band improvised extensively. It was largely due to this that they had stayed away from live releases, believing that every gig was unique and live albums weren't really capable of representing the band as accurately as they would have liked. Because the beauty of Purple is largely based around the popularity of its live performances, and in particular the improvisations, this is a view that generally leaves fans baffled. One look at the large amount of bootlegs that exist and the number of fans that collect these live recordings is evidence that Deep Purple's live work is the true representation of the group's sound. Their studio work, whilst producing many great compositions, often failed to capture the essence of that unique 'live' sound they were constantly striving for.

But live albums were not as common in the early seventies as they are today. Cream had produced it's 'Wheels Of Fire' album recorded at the Fillmore East in the late sixties, and by 1970 The Who had produced 'Live At Leeds,' but the bands that would become such a dominant force in the early seventies, acts such as Black Sabbath, Led Zeppelin and of course Deep Purple, paid little attention to releasing live records. By the time Purple eventually succumbed to the idea of producing a live record they already had six studio albums under their belt. Of course, had things gone to plan in Switzerland the previous December, 'Machine Head' might well have been a double album combining the studio record alongside a live one they planned to record at the Montreux Casino. Once Deep Purple had agreed to Warner Brothers' idea they were adamant that, if the gigs were going to be recorded, this should be done properly. As such, their trustworthy engineer Martin Birch was employed to record the shows.

With no overdubs of any kind, the best performances from Martin Birch's superb recordings were picked and mixed by Roger Glover and Ian Paice. Birch recalled that the others showed little interest in the recordings: "Neither Ian nor Ritchie turned up to listen to the play-back. I'm not sure whether either of them ever listened to the album all the way through." But for those who did listen to the recordings they were so taken aback by the quality that what was originally planned solely for the Japanese market was given the go ahead for worldwide release. By this stage in the band's career, Martin Birch had fully established himself as almost a sixth member of the band and his contributions to the finished sound should not be overlooked. For both the studio recordings and the Japanese recordings that would become the live masterpiece 'Made In Japan,' much of the credit should go to Birch for producing such a fabulous sound.

When putting the album together, the tracks were mainly taken from the second Osaka show. The reasoning behind this showed that, once the band were fully behind the concept, they were adamant that they wanted it to be as good as possible. It had been considered that the first night's performance was generally slightly below the standard the band expected of itself due to the fact they had just arrived the day before and were still recovering from jetlag. But the immortal 'Smoke On The Water' from that opening night's gig did make it onto the record. Although two tracks from the Tokyo show were also included, the band were generally unhappy with the acoustics on the recording, and this is why the rest of the album is from the second night in Osaka.

With no let-up in the schedule, it was back to America for the rest of August and early September. Although the recordings in Japan suggested a band at the peak of its ability, the relationship between Blackmore and Gillan continued to fester: much of this stemmed form Gillan's insistence on travelling on the American tours with his girlfriend, Zoë Dean. The rest of the guys were enjoying the rock 'n' roll lifestyle to the max. Groupies were in abundance and were literally throwing themselves at rock stars. In general it seemed that the bigger the stars were, the more women there were to offer their 'services.'

With Deep Purple now one of the biggest bands on the planet, American tours were a joy for virile young men. With wives and girlfriends back at home in England, the chance to indulge in a daily offering of 'extra-curricular activity' was welcome for any man with a libido to match. Blackmore in particular was very much into entertaining female fans, but the presence of Zoë was something that neither he nor the rest of the guys were particularly enamoured with. Ian Gillan also started to play the star part and, as Lord said to Swedish journalist Mike Eriksson in 1981, "Ian was a primadonna. On stage he played a primadonna and offstage he was a primadonna." Ian Gillan soon became more isolated from the rest of the band and started travelling independently. He hired his own personal roadie, Ossy Hoppe, but whether he was pushed into this or chose it of his own accord is something that to this day none of the band has been prepared to elaborate on.

Outside of the personal problems surrounding the band, Glover and Paice's friends Elf joined Purple for this American tour, promoting the debut album that Glover and Paice had produced. Elf would probably have been oblivious to the frictions in the band they were now touring with. In fact it was only towards the end of this tour that long-standing roadie Ian Hansford started to pick up on the bad vibes: "I can remember Ritchie just took his guitar off half way through a number, it was the end of the set anyway and he threw it on the floor and walked off. He didn't lay it down, just got hold of it by the neck and slammed it on the floor. Apparently Ian Gillan said to him, 'look at me you cunt.' He was like leading it and Ritchie took umbrage to that and took his guitar off and threw it on the floor and went." Hansford eventually found Blackmore back at the hotel. "I just said to him, 'what the hell was going on I've been looking for you I didn't know where you were.' He just said, 'I'm sorry, I've just had it with Gillan basically.' After that life did get a bit fraught. It was like trying to keep them apart basically. If one were getting away with one thing the other would try and get away with something else. It was just an ongoing battle."

With no chance for a break it was straight back to the UK to commence another tour on 13th September. This tour was notable for Purple's appearance as the launch gig for the Brixton Sundown, a venue that had previously been a cinema and is now known as the Brixton Academy. The tour concluded at Croydon's Fairfield Hall on 8th October and, following a couple of gigs in France, the band's next duty was to complete their new album. This time they chose a small studio in a village just outside Frankfurt in Germany, and even though the bitterness was still in the air a more professional approach was adopted. As Glover described it, "generally there was a quiet determination to make up for time spent doing very little on what was now regarded as our summer holiday in Italy. Despite the smooth progress not all was healthy with the band dynamic; rarely would we all be in the same room at the same time." Glover himself arrived late for the first day's work as a result of missing the turn off on the autobahn. With the bass player absent, Lord and Paice kicked off a jam with Blackmore joining in on Glover's Rickenbacker bass. This eleven-minute jam was indicative of the way that Purple's ideas came together, but it was also a rarity to have Blackmore playing the bass guitar. The recording eventually saw the light of day on the re-mastered edition of the album it relates to in 2000.

Glover also recalled that he was now employed as a conduit between Blackmore and Gillan. "I never spoke to Ian Gillan all that time we made that LP," admitted Blackmore a couple of years later. The others also experienced Blackmore's reluctance to co-operate with the rest of the band, and his apparent enthusiasm for Deep Purple in general seemed to be at an all-time low. During the sessions he sometimes came up with ideas that the band latched onto, only to tell them that he was saving them for his solo album. It was probably the project he had in mind with Phil Lynott that he was referring to. "Everybody refused to write with everybody else, I was even holding back ideas. I'm not going to give Purple this idea, because this is for another thing, so I was turning out shit and so was everyone else. It was rubbish," Blackmore later admitted. Despite the divisions in the band, Martin Birch didn't see any direct antagonism, in fact far from it: "The only noticeable thing would be that Ian Gillan possibly wouldn't come into the sessions when Ritchie was doing his stuff and vice versa. So Ritchie would do some solos, they'd lay the track down, Ritchie would perhaps stick some guitar on – Ian wouldn't see it. By the time it came to the vocals Ian would come in, possibly Roger, and do his vocals and then Ritchie would appear at the end of the track when it was all finished and listen to it without Ian there, and that's how it worked so there was never any confrontation that I saw as that would have been destructive towards the actual making of the album."

"There was a sadness around these final days of the project that was occasionally relieved by the music, which continued to generate the familiar magic," remembers Glover. Glover shows that, despite the misery surrounding the album, his views on the end results were far more positive than Blackmore's. However, shortly after the album was completed, with the band back on the road in America, Ian Gillan informed the management of his intention to quit the band. Initially Edwards and Coletta tried to persuade him to re-consider, although they seemed more concerned with ensuring he didn't walk out of a band that had months of concert commitments lined-up. They also got an agreement from Ian Gillan that he wouldn't make any public announcements about his intention. At least with the live recordings mixed, whatever the future held for Deep Purple or

what the band's views were on the 'Who Do We Think We Are' album, they could at least present a united front to the fans for the impending live release.

When 'Made In Japan' was released in December '72, it was the finest advert imaginable for anyone who had not seen Deep Purple in concert, and made sure that they purchased a ticket the next time the band came to town. It perfectly illustrates how the studio compositions were transformed within the concert arena. As an analogy, it's like the difference between watching a film on a giant cinema screen with surround sound compared to a mobile phone! Even listening to the album today, thirty-five years after it was recorded, it still packs a mean punch. It's hard to imagine all these years on just how significant 'Made In Japan' was for rock audiences of the time. Given that the early seventies saw a glut of superb classic rock bands performing to their absolute peak in concert halls throughout the world, it's incredible to think that documenting live performances was always given short shrift by most bands. The success of 'Made In Japan' really paved the way for the double live albums that followed. As the seventies progressed, other bands such as Thin Lizzy and UFO produced some of their finest moments in the same format. Despite Jimmy Page's fussiness, even Led Zeppelin managed to release a double live LP, but no one other than the most hardened Zeppelin fan could consider that it came remotely close to eclipsing 'Made In Japan.'

Having shown little interest in the project, it was only Ian Gillan who had reservations about the album. Having just recovered from a bout of bronchitis before the trip to Japan he was unhappy with his own performances. But fans were hard pushed to share Ian Gillan's criticism. He proved with 'Child In Time' that not only could he replicate the amazing vocal performance from the 'In Rock' album, but that he could take it to new heights as well. It seems obvious now that such a classic live album had to include 'Smoke On The Water,' and listening to the album today it's quite comical to think that Ian Gillan actually introduces the song by name, as if it needed any introduction. But at the time of the recording, 'Smoke On The Water' was just another song in the show, which also explains why it was played so early in the set. The version captured on the album deviates from that unique and undeniably simple opening riff that Blackmore plays. Perhaps even this early on in the song's life, Blackmore felt the need to chop and change it to stop himself from getting bored. Whether or not that is the case, it's another example of the way Purple songs could vary so much in the live arena. Also, as is the case with live recordings, songs that otherwise fade out on their studio recordings have different endings worked out for the stage. For 'Smoke On The Water,' Jon Lord brings the organ solo to a conclusion with the greatest of Purple trademarks as he and Blackmore throw the riffs back and forth before Paice and Glover pound out the closing notes. This live version helped to elevate the popularity of the song, particularly in America, and Warner released a double A-side single the following year that included both the 'Machine Head' version and the live version from 'Made In Japan.' 'Smoke On The Water' was a massive stateside hit and has become one of the most enduring and well-known rock songs of all time.

In keeping with the traditions of the day, no live rock show in 1972 would be complete without a drum solo. 'The Mule' taken from the 'Fireball' album was greatly revamped in order to use it as a showcase for Ian Paice's drum solo. It might seem odd to throw a drum solo into the middle of a track like 'The Mule,' but 'Paint It Black' had been used for the same purpose until replaced, which helps to put the decision in context. Lengthy drum solos were considered quite acceptable in the early seventies, and with Ian Paice being one of rock's finest drummers of the day, it made perfect sense to have his skills permanently captured on record. It is also worth mentioning that Paice was never one to use an over-sized kit. For example, all the footwork is done with just one bass drum!

For some, the album's stand out track was 'Strange Kind Of Woman.' Taking a three-minute hit single and turning it into a ten-minute tour de force was typical of the enormous changes Purple's music would undergo in order to relate it to a live audience that clamoured to hear musicians showing their skills to the maximum. Not only were Blackmore's two solos extended far beyond the studio version, but the most dramatic section of the song was the guitar / vocal interplay, which became one of the most exciting parts of the show. Ian Gillan, at the height of his talents, producing superb interpretations of Blackmore's guitar notes was a highlight of the live show and also became a hugely exciting Deep Purple trademark. No matter what Blackmore played, the vocalist seemed capable of reproducing it. Finally Gillan stamps his identity on the closing moments of the song in his most distinguishable and unique fashion, with his astonishing screams. It was elements such as these that made Purple stand out from most of the other bands of the day. Certainly there were few bands that had a singer capable of matching Gillan's dynamics, and 'Strange Kind Of Woman' is indeed a testimony to this. Interestingly, the guitar / vocal interplay had originally developed naturally on stage during 'Demon's Eye,' but as that song was swiftly removed from the set list it found a new home in 'Strange Kind Of Woman' where it remained for the rest of the stage shelf life.

Whilst 'Strange Kind Of Woman' showcased the vocalist and guitarist, 'Lazy' was an important number for Jon Lord. Fans who were familiar with the earlier live sets from the group will spot the similarities in the structure and rhythm to the lengthy instrumental 'Wring That Neck,' and 'Lazy' was ideal for the live show once 'Wring That Neck' had been dropped. In keeping with the original studio version, 'Lazy' opens with a solo organ; but in a live show, Lord's work was full of new inventions that once again would differ on a nightly basis, with all sorts of weird and wonderful sounds emanating from his keyboards. With the back of the Hammond organ removed, exposing its workings, Lord would sometimes poke a drum stick inside it, producing some very unique and heavily distorted sounds. Eventually he would kick into the main melody as the cue for the rest of the band to join in. Although essentially a blues-based piece, there were also Jazz inflections thrown in. Ian Paice adapted the drumming accordingly due to his formative years playing swing in his father's big band.

Like 'Lazy,' 'Space Truckin'' was also a great addition to the live set once the older songs were replaced. It became the set closer, taking over from 'Mandrake Root,' which had been in the live show from the very first gig back in 1968. In essence, much of the live structures of 'Mandrake Root' were incorporated into 'Space Truckin'.' In fact 'Space Truckin'' was, to all intents and purposes, the welding together of the studio song with the live structures of 'Mandrake Root.' Performing the first few minutes much like the studio version from 'Machine Head,' it then changed tempo with Paice and Glover setting down a solid rhythm over which Lord and Blackmore would solo at length. A fast flurry of notes taken from 'Mandrake Root' was used as Lord's 'check out' that Blackmore would also play alongside, before taking over the soloing. The solos would vary nightly from hard and aggressive to very quiet and melancholy passages, as with Blackmore's work that was captured on the 'Made In Japan' version. His volume control technique that formed the central section of 'Fools' on the 'Fireball' album had originally been developed on stage during 'Mandrake Root,' and consequently it was incorporated into 'Space Truckin'' as was perfectly illustrated on 'Made In Japan.'

But if anything it was the opening cut 'Highway Star' that set the standards few bands could only dream of. In Roger Glover's words 'Highway Star' was "the ultimate Deep Purple track" and it isn't difficult to see why. It's a perfect example of a band in total harmony, playing at its formidable best. Ian Paice's drumming sets a solid foundation while at the same time his exuberant style sees him throwing in fills wherever he can. Roger Glover's thunderous bass drives the song along, whilst the classic solos from Lord and Blackmore are without doubt the icing on the cake. A more perfect example of power rock you couldn't wish to hear. Interestingly given that Blackmore was renowned for changing his solos night by night, such was the classic structure of 'Highway Star' that it was one of the few tracks where the original studio solo was pretty much replicated the same on stage, albeit with so much more vibrancy than the studio version and with an astonishing show of speed and dexterity.

Not only did 'Made In Japan' act as a great advert for Deep Purple's awesome live performances, but also, more by design than accident, releasing a live record at that moment in time deflected from the audiences' clamour for a new studio album, something the band had struggled to produce due to the ever-growing tensions. When 'Made In Japan' was released just in time for the Christmas market, the double live release also helped to hide the disharmony in the ranks from an eager public, and showed the band firing on all cylinders. However, the release of the album also coincided with Ian Gillan confirming his decision to resign following a letter written on 9th December after a gig in Dayton, Ohio, although the news would be kept from the public for several months. Gillan clarified his dissatisfaction with his own position, as well as his disillusionment with what he saw as the continuing stagnation of Deep Purple's own existence. The concerns about future commitments were overcome as Gillan agreed to see out the gigs through to the band's second Japanese tour in June 1973. The rest of the band were immediately informed of Gillan's decision, and what had already developed into a fairly tense situation only got worse now that the band was confronted with having to work alongside a vocalist who no longer wished to be a part of their group.

Rumours of a split had been doing the rounds in the music press for months, and as far back as April Jon Lord had commented, "it could last another three years or it could last another three months; you never know when a group is at this stage. It might just get to the stage where somebody thinks they'd rather be doing something else. I don't think the group would continue if one person left. I'd be able to tell you better if it happened but I think we'd call it a day." But by December, it was announced that 'Machine Head' had gone Gold in the UK and, with Purple now at a commercial peak, for the band to have just called it a day would have been ludicrous from a financial perspective. But apart from Gillan's now internally confirmed departure, it was apparent that Blackmore also remained keen to pursue his project with Phil Lynott. The management was eager to see the band continue and, seeing that they could also lose Blackmore, they were greatly concerned that Deep Purple could fold after only five years together. It was initially put to Lord and Glover to see if they could hold the band together. Concerned that Ian Paice may also jump ship with Blackmore, they urged the keyboard player and bassist to try and talk Paice into staying as well. Roger Glover said: "It was popularly supposed that sooner or later Ritchie was going to leave and take Ian Paice with him. Ian Gillan had already announced his intention to leave and so there was a feeling of doom about the band at that time. The next I heard about it we were on tour in America. We sort of agreed to try and keep the band going despite Ritchie's imminent departure, and Ian Gillan's."

The next few months would prove to be the most fraught within the band's history, as the internal strife would also be matched by troubles that arose at some of the gigs. At the De Oude Rai in Amsterdam on 28th January 1973, violence erupted amongst the audience on a scale unlike anything Deep Purple had witnessed before. Not only had the band arrived late from Cologne, but once they got there they took an instant dislike to the venue. "It was like an old railway station or something. It was a massive place," recalls Purple roadie Ian Hansford. Besides the fact that the venue not ideally suited for concerts, there was also a problem with the power supply; concerns over the lack of security also threatened the cancellation of the show. Blackmore in particular seemed concerned with the lack of organisation and the apparent over-crowding of the venue.

When the start of the show was delayed, the crowd became restless and some of them took to throwing beer cans at the stage. Deep Purple eventually took to the stage an hour later than scheduled, but the show was cut short when one of Blackmore's guitar strings broke. He threw the guitar in the air and promptly left the stage. The band had only been playing for fifty-five minutes, but with no guitarist the rest of the band soon followed. Roger Glover said, "I'll never come back here. This is complete madness with all these people here. I was too frightened to be on stage."

Unfortunately the audience didn't take kindly to being short-changed, and following an announcement that the show was over the crowd became even more restless. Much confusion resulted with the house lights being turned on and then back off again, and probably in an attempt to quell the anger another announcement was made that one more song would be performed, but the band had no intention of going back on stage. By the time the house lights went on again the crowd was seething and once again peppered the stage with beer cans. Before long a tower of speakers was pushed over after which many of the audience jumped on the stage and a full-scale destruction ensued. With minimal security on hand to control the crowd, Purple's road crew were left to ward off the rioters armed with microphone stands, seriously injuring some of them in the process. It was almost two in the morning before the crowd was finally dispersed from the hall. "The PA got smashed," remembers Hansford. "I don't recall why it kicked off but I seem to remember that for the next gig they had to bring out a new PA system for us. I remember Rob Cooksey saying after it, 'I don't want to ever go through that again'". The following day one of Purple's road managers, Nick Dorman, surprisingly attached some of the blame to the band: "The band is partly to blame for not playing an encore. They should have known it would end in a riot. A few days ago we played in Germany. They refused to play an encore as well and the German audience wasn't too pleased neither, but we managed to leave without any damage." In Amsterdam most of the equipment was trashed and, with another gig planned for three days time in Copenhagen, new equipment was immediately ordered from Marshall's in London.

'Who Do We Think We Are' was released in the UK in March '73 and it is generally considered the weakest of the MKII albums. But even though some are quick to dismiss it, the album is by no means a disaster and it certainly has its moments. Lyrically 'Mary Long' was a radical song and without doubt the most political number Purple wrote during this period. Gillan's lyrics targeted the 'so-called' moral majority, spearheaded by the 'clean-up' campaigner Mary Whitehouse and 'do-gooders' like Lord Longford, who at the time was campaigning for parole for the moor's murderess, Myra Hindley. Longford argued that Hindley, and indeed all offenders, could be rehabilitated if society was prepared to forgive. However, it was the crusade against pornography that Longford embarked upon under the influence of Mary Whitehouse and anti-libertarians that was the central issue for the lyrics. Whilst Longford aimed to outlaw pornography, touring the sex clubs that he wanted to close down in order to get a better understanding of what they represented showed him to be a prurient reactionary and a shameless hypocrite. Apart from a couple of anti-drug songs on 'In Rock,' Deep Purple wasn't renowned for preaching messages of any kind. Even Blackmore has cited 'Mary Long' as one of the best tracks on the album, which perhaps explains why it was the only song from the album that was performed live during the European tour at the beginning of the year. Pornographic film projections were also used during the performance to convey the message within the lyrics. 'Smooth Dancer' was another song where the lyrics overshadowed the music. Due to the clever way Gillan had written it, reviewers didn't exactly latch on to the fact that he was singing about his relationship and thoughts on Ritchie Blackmore. "You can rock 'n' roll but you can never show your soul" and "you're swollen up inside with nothing but your pride" were vicious attacks on Blackmore's character. As Blackmore claimed to show little interest in the lyrics, it's doubtful that even he was aware at the time of what Ian Gillan was singing about.

For those who thought that Purple was a spent force at this stage, 'Place In Line' is by far and away one of the most imaginative pieces on the album. Although it is based around a simple blues structure, it is a sadly overlooked gem from Purple MKII's output and a personal favourite of the author. Ian Gillan's unique vocals on the verses sound totally unlike anything he has done before or since, and the whole thing really kicks off once the change of tempo introduces the chorus before settling down to let Blackmore and Lord deliver fabulous solos of the highest calibre.

The album's opening cut 'Woman From Tokyo' was a favourite for most listeners and reviewers, so it was no surprise that it was chosen as a single. In order to make it palatable for daytime radio, Ian Paice's editing reduced it to a shadow of the album track. The single was released throughout Europe, but although a catalogue number was also assigned for a UK release, for reasons unexplained it never materialised. For those countries that did get the single, they also got a previously unreleased live version of 'Black Night' on the b-side, the encore from Tokyo '72 taken from the recordings for 'Made In Japan.'

Arguably the weakest track on the album is 'Our Lady,' which comes across as a poor attempt at trying to make a commercial hit single. As Jon Lord described it at the time, "it's very slow and concentrates more on the tune and the lyrics." It's indicative of Ian Paice's belief that they were "finding it harder to come up with killer riffs." It's probably no coincidence that such a weak track was to be the last MKII track committed to vinyl as the band was clearly in need of some rejuvenation. However, this shouldn't overshadow the vast bulk of the work that this classic line-up left as a legacy. Incidentally, the title idea for this particular song came from Ritchie Blackmore after he walked past a church with this name!

The American tour that kicked off in April and took the band through to mid June would prove to be the toughest the band would undertake. Sound engineer Bob Simon recalled how fraught things were between Gillan and Blackmore: "probably the third tour I did with them they were completely on different trips. There wasn't much socialising between them." According to Roger Glover, "the last year I don't think Ritchie and Ian Gillan spoke one word to each other." Blackmore was still in two minds whether or not to continue with the band or depart and do his own thing. Once Ian Paice had decided that it was

132

in his own interest to carry on watching the money roll in with Deep Purple, he was left with the job of convincing Blackmore to stay. Blackmore eventually agreed, but in an unexpected turnaround, he did so only on the condition that Glover was replaced. "I wanted to form this thing with Phil Lynott," he explained a decade ago. "I said I wanted to leave, and Ian Paice said: 'Could anything persuade you to stay, because we're on to such a good thing. Why mess it up?' I said: 'No, I want to get together with Phil, myself, you. It will be a great band. I want to do a bluesier thing.' But I also had hesitations – and I think Phil did too because he was doing well. We wanted to play together but he'd just had a hit (Whiskey In The Jar). But Paicey was reluctant to leave."

With Blackmore's visions of a bluesier band, he considered that Glover's bass playing wasn't suitable for what he had in mind. Seeing that Blackmore was more crucial to the band's ongoing success, Paice and Lord agreed to go along with the guitarist's wishes. Given that, after Blackmore, Glover was the next major composer within the band, the desire to split with a major song-writing asset on the strength of his bass playing certainly seemed like an odd decision. It's quite feasible that what was playing on Blackmore's mind was the opportunity to dominate the group's song writing. With the records selling by the millions, and the biggest chunk of the income coming from publishing, with Glover and Gillan out of the equation Blackmore could in effect mould the band exactly to his requirements. Surrendering musical partnerships of the calibre that Lord and Paice offered was also something that no wise man would want to do lightly.

Years later, Ian Gillan reflected on the break up of the band: "We were all kids that had never experienced this before even though we were pretty hard-nosed pros by then and we hadn't had to deal with things at this level and at the time you have to sacrifice a lot of your own personal integrity up to a point and doing things you don't want to do for the sake of the 'business.' I think we were tired and in need of a break but it all got pretty hairy and we broke up."

Even with Gillan's lengthy notice there appeared to be little urgency in seeking a replacement, and only two possible candidates were considered. Paul Rodgers was always first on Ritchie Blackmore's list. Rodger's band Free had been through some rough times and had split up in April '71, only to reform early the following year. Andy Fraser soon quit after that, and Paul Kossoff's drug habit caused immense problems for the band. By early '73, Free had called a halt on proceedings for good. However, although Rodgers was free to join Deep Purple (pun intended), it was unclear whether or not he was interested. Along with Free drummer Simon Kirke he had aspirations to try and develop something new. The other singer who had caught their attention was Glenn Hughes, bassist and vocalist with the Midlands outfit Trapeze. Blackmore, Lord and Paice had originally seen Trapeze in America in late '72. Back in England in early '73, Trapeze played four nights at London's Marquee club between 8th January and 23rd March and again members of Deep Purple were in the audience for one of these gigs. They were impressed with Hughes, although as much for his bass playing as his singing, even though the decision to dispense with Glover hadn't been made at this point.

Glenn Hughes was born in Cannock, Staffordshire on 21st August 1952 and had music in his blood. His first band involvement was as early as 1965 with the Hooker Lees. Taking the name from blues guitarist John Lee Hooker, one would be forgiven in thinking the band was performing Negro blues, but in truth Rolling Stones covers were more in evidence (although The Stones had clearly taken their cues from Negro blues artists such as Hooker and, more obviously, Muddy Waters).

The Hooker Lees changed their name to The Intruders, but Hughes quickly moved on to another band called The News, where he was both lead guitarist and vocalist. By 1968 he had joined Finders Keepers, where he made his recording debut on backing vocals for the group's one and only single that was all but completed before Hughes had joined. Towards the end of the year Hughes formed Trapeze along with guitarist Mel Galley and drummer Dave Holland. They recruited a vocalist in John Jones and also had Terry Rowley on organ. By 1970 Trapeze had been signed to the Moody Blues Threshold label and released its self-titled debut album. Rowley and Jones departed soon after its release and, with the band stripped down to a trio, Hughes took over lead vocals. A second and much stronger album 'Medusa' was released later the same year. The band's third release, 'You Are The Music ... We're Just The Band,' proved to be Trapeze's strongest album and things really kicked off for Trapeze in America following a tour supporting The Moody Blues. Their popularity increased enormously, particularly in the Southern States, and they were soon playing to large audiences in Tennessee and Texas, while still performing club venues like the Marquee back in Britain.

With Blackmore, Lord and Paice showing up at several Trapeze gigs, Hughes eventually started to sense they were checking him out, although it certainly took a while for the penny to drop, as he explained to the author in 2005: "I was pretty slow to understand because I was so young and so naïve that I just thought they liked the band. Lordy & Paicey would come one night and Ritchie would always come alone or with his wife. Maybe the third time I figured something's up here. I think it was the last time Ritchie came to see me. They'd seen me twice in LA at the Whisky, and then Ritchie came again in London and Jon again in London at the Marquee. It was then that I started to realise and I'd heard a rumour that Gillan was leaving. All along I never realised they wanted me to take Roger's place; I thought they just wanted me to be the singer."

Despite the fact that in the last few months the MKII line-up were soldiering on, audiences would have been oblivious to the internal discord. During the final American tour in May, ABC TV filmed a gig at Hofstra University in New York. Although ABC filmed the entire show, it was edited into a 25 minute broadcast and sadly, as was so typical of the times, the complete, unedited reels were re-used! However, what footage remains is a superb example of Deep Purple on stage. The most interesting thing about this footage is the on stage atmosphere. Given the disharmony that was festering within the band at this stage, they gave no indication of this to the audience. In fact the band looks like it was having a whale of a time, and bearing in mind that a month later MKII would conclude with a last gig in Japan, the on stage banter is quite astonishing.

However, although Ian Gillan's performance showed a man who looked happy that his tenure was coming to an end, for Roger Glover it would be later in the tour before he actually realised that something was afoot. "During that tour, I think it was in Jacksonville, I certainly became aware of a coldness towards me from the others. I just didn't feel included anymore in discussions. There was no conversation directed my way and it's little pointers like that, that make you feel uneasy. I finally prized it out of Tony Edwards after the show. I went to his room and said, 'what's up?' He said, 'nothing,' but I knew something was up and I refused to leave his room until he told me, and he said, basically the deal is this. Ritchie will stay in the band as long as I left but they didn't want to tell me because they wanted me to complete the tour, so I handed in my notice, very sadly. I certainly don't want to be in a band that doesn't want me and the rest of that tour was uncomfortable, I went through many emotions."

After discovering his fate in Jacksonville, Glover had to endure two shows in Florida, one in Georgia and, to round the US tour off, a gig in Hawaii. The Hawaiian capital of Honolulu was an ideal end of tour venue, allowing the band to break up the long journey for the remaining few MKII dates in Japan. Unlike a year earlier, the Japanese gigs didn't have the same enjoyable atmosphere that had been portrayed on the 'Made In Japan' recordings. The show at Tokyo's Budokan was marred by rioting after Blackmore chose not to do an encore. Photos of the venue with a sea of demolished seating have been used in several sleeve designs and publications on the band, and help to convey the audience's annoyance. Soundman Bob Simon will never forget the events that kicked off once the crowd realised the band wasn't going to return after finishing the main set with 'Space Truckin.' "I'm back in the hotel finally a couple of hours later, and I'm on the elevator, getting to my room. My clothes are all tore up, I'm all bloody and I've been fighting with all these Jap guys and Ritchie's getting out of the elevator and I said to him, 'what the fuck was that all about?' Because he didn't want to do an encore: He said, 'The audience sucked. They didn't deserve an encore so fuck 'em.' But we had just taken a good bollocking and all the equipment got busted up. He liked to see things happening."

While fans smashed up the venue in Tokyo, at the final gig at the Koseinenkin in Osaka on 29th June 1973, it was the band that trashed their own equipment. German photographer Didi Zill, who had been taking photos of the band for the past three years, primarily for Germany's Bravo magazine, captured the scene perfectly. At the end of the gig, Zill snapped a shot of Ian Paice's drum kit strewn all over the place, and a blanket of dry ice smoke forming a thick covering across the stage floor. Roger Glover stood in front of his amps, with his bass guitar in hand. The only other member of the band on stage was Ian Gillan. Both men were surveying the scene for the last time, undoubtedly with mixed emotions. For Gillan, the elevation to Purple had seen egos and bank balances soar and relationships decline. For Glover, a forced departure meant that a writing partnership with his long time friend that had started in Episode Six was now redundant. Before leaving the stage, Ian Gillan gave a farewell speech: "All I want to say to all of you is thank you very much – you are great. Thank you for everything you have given us in Japan and thank you, really, for the representatives of the whole world as far as we are concerned. Thank you and God bless you for everything you have ever given us. And this is the last night, the end. God bless you, thanks a lot."

- CHAPTER FIVE -
SOLDIERS OF FORTUNE

GIVEN THAT Ian Gillan had given the band nine months' notice of his departure, it might seem odd that no one was ready to step into his role following the last gig. Glenn Hughes had already been notified of his appointment to the band as Glover's replacement, and although his initial assumption was that he would be the sole vocalist as well, he appeared more than happy to combine the dual role with bass playing. This was helped because the one man that Blackmore had in mind as lead vocalist was Paul Rodgers, a singer of immense quality who was greatly admired by Hughes. If Purple could secure Rodgers they would be getting two world-class vocalists for the price of one. "When Ian left it was an enormous gap to fill – we had to find the kind of singer who could carry that weight on his shoulders. So the guy we obviously thought of was Paul Rodgers," said Blackmore. Rodgers had certainly built up a reputation over the past five years as one of Britain's finest rock singers during his time as front man with blues based Free. With Blackmore's desire to steer Purple into a bluesier direction, Rodgers would have been ideal for the role. However, Paul Rodgers had other ideas. His stature had grown to the point where joining an established band just wasn't as appealing as creating his own, new band. Like Blackmore, Rodgers has a reputation as something of a control freak and, despite leaked press reports that he was to join Deep Purple, Rodgers turned down the invitation before even having a blow with the band. Instead, along with Free's Simon Kirke, he focused on creating a new band

and by the end of '73 Bad Company was born. Not only was Deep Purple left with egg on its face, but this also meant they were back to square one and left with the unenviable task of placing adverts in the music press, just like they had done when they got Rod Evans five years earlier.

However, by now Purple was a globally successful band and they were quite simply inundated with tapes by established singers and would be superstars. Wading though the tapes that arrived at the management's London office was a turgid time for the remaining members. "When it became known that we were looking for a new singer we were swamped with tapes. We tried to listen but we really had a hard time finding anything decent," recalled Lord. Fortunately John Coletta did much of the pruning. "About forty tapes were sent to me," said Coletta. "I went through them and whittled it down and played them to Jon, Ian and Ritchie."

Eventually they played a tape that actually impressed them. It was from an unknown semi-pro singer from North East England called David Coverdale. "Auditioning a singer wasn't really difficult because there was only ever one guy we auditioned, David Coverdale. I think the other guys were listening to hundreds of cassettes of singers," explained Glenn Hughes in recent years. Hughes's comment is a little wide of the mark, as Coletta recalled that quite a few guys were actually auditioned at a place called Scorpio Sound in Marylebone Road under the Capital Radio Studios in central London. It could well be that some auditions were held before Hughes joined the original trio, or simply that his memory has failed him. To those who were invited down for an audition, they had no idea they were applying for the role of lead singer in one of the biggest bands in the world. "It was quite a shock for them," recalled Coletta. "None of these people knew what they were walking into. They thought it was a band just starting up

or even a little way up the ladder, but not something as big as Purple," he explained.

Ian Paice recalled the moment he first heard Coverdale's tape: "David's tape was rubbish except for four bars where he actually sung really hard and I thought there was something in his voice that was really good, so I said let's get him down here. He had these incredibly awful glasses on and this strange, not quite straight hair, and he had an eye that wandered around. I'm sure it was a nervous thing and he was massively overweight but we got him in the studio and he sang very well. But part of the deal was, if you are going to come into the band, you've got to look a bit different to that, because he looked exactly what he was, a chap from a clothing store who really didn't give a toss about himself. He agreed to everything because he wanted in and became the glorious David Coverdale that everybody knows and loves today."

David Coverdale remembered the process later: "I sent a tape and a photograph down, asking if I could have the job basically! I was working in a shop and I didn't expect to get the job with Purple. If I got an audition, I was hoping ... I knew they had their own record label, I was hoping they could offer me something on my own or say, 'look your voice isn't the sort of voice we are looking for but we know someone who is.' But after blowing with the band I couldn't believe it, I went apeshit, I couldn't sleep. I'd always worked with good musicians but this was like another level. It was so in tune with what I wanted and fortunately it was what they wanted so it worked out well. But it was the first time I had got off my arse to do something and it paid off."

David Coverdale was born on 22nd September 1951 in Saltburn-by-the-Sea, North Yorkshire. Having been plucked from obscurity, naturally his musical career was far less spectacular than any of the other band members. His parents operated a small club in the town and the Coverdale family lived in the accommodation above it. With a jukebox in the club, these surroundings helped to introduce the youngster to the happening sixties music. Jimi Hendrix soon became a firm favourite and fights broke out at the local youth club as young Coverdale regularly fought to get his selections on the record player. Although he taught himself to play guitar he soon veered towards singing. After leaving school Coverdale enrolled at an art college in Middlesbrough, where he soon got to meet fellow musicians. By 1967 he had helped to form a band called Denver Mule who managed a few gigs over the next year or so. The ironically named Purple Onion Coffee Bar was a regular social gathering venue, and it was there that Coverdale met a young guitarist called Mickey Moody from a band called Tramline that had secured a record deal with Island Records. Coverdale occasionally helped out as a roadie, but he had clearly set his sights higher. When the irregular Denver Mule split, Coverdale managed to get a gig with The Skyliners. Although the band was only semi-pro, Coverdale jacked in college to focus on the group full-time. They were earning enough money that he could afford to do so, although the rest of the band continued to keep their day jobs.

The Skyliners changed its name to The Government in 1969, but the major drawback for Coverdale was the band's 'double life.' The group had to flit between shaping a set for the cabaret scene and their preferred style of rock for the university fraternity in order to get a sufficient amount of gigs. At one of the latter style gigs, they even supported Deep Purple at Bradford University on 22nd November 1969. Ian Gillan had only been in the band for a few months at that stage, but clearly Jon Lord must have felt that it wasn't inevitable that Gillan would shape up. Lord asked for Coverdale's address and number. "Jon said if things didn't work out with Gillan he might give me a call," claimed

Coverdale. Fans can decide for themselves as to whether or not Lord and Co. did the right thing in not contacting Coverdale again! As the seventies kicked off, The Government started to play the big hit sounds of the day, including Black Sabbath's 'Paranoid,' and they even did a version of 'Black Night.' By 1971 they pondered whether or not to turn professional and, despite the fact that they decided against it, they did at least cut a four-track EP, although only a few copies were pressed up for friends and relatives, making it one of the rarest recordings to feature any Deep Purple member. With insufficient money coming in, Coverdale had no option but to take a day job and chose shop work selling men's clothes at the local boutique. When gigs were available the evenings would be spent singing in a Santana style group called River's Invitation. By early '73 he had put a four-piece together to perform at a local charity gig, billing the band as The Fabulosa Brothers. It developed into a once a week gig at a local pub, while the day job kept up a steady income.

Needless to say, for a young semi-pro vocalist plucked from obscurity, David Coverdale's audition was a moment in his life he will never forget: "Paicey and Lordy were already at the studio when I arrived ... Mr. Lord was exceptionally charming and welcoming, doing his best to put me at ease, while Ian messed around on his Ludwig drumkit. Ritchie arrived next ... He completely ignored me, other than a quick surreptitious look to check me out ... a brief nod when we made eye contact. Without missing a beat I was off to the whiskey for a quick, nervous sip. Glenn was late and came tumbling into the studio with all his baggage, sunglasses falling off, laughing like a madman. He apologised to everyone for being late then proceeded to take his beautiful red Rickenbacker bass out of its case. Glenn was one of the most natural musicians I've ever worked with. I never, ever saw him practice. When it came time to work he simply picked up his instrument, and played flawlessly every time. Slowly, but surely they all started to play and lo and behold they were jamming on grooves – not Purple songs just cool grooves, making it up as they went along."

Coverdale had bought a couple of the albums and was expecting them to try him out on the group's own repertoire. Even though he was undeniably nervous, Coverdale did tell the lads that he had learnt 'Strange Kind Of Woman,' and they soon did a run through of it after which Coverdale recalls Blackmore saying, "Okay, you can sing rock, let's see what you can do with a ballad. Anything you want to sing?" "Do you know the Beatles song 'Yesterday' in 'F'?" I asked. Coverdale is of the opinion that it was the ability to sing the ballad that was the key to his appointment. "I'm not sure but I think that one actually got me the gig."

The search for a replacement vocalist had also given Purple a lengthy, unexpected break, which was nevertheless a welcome one from the rigours of endless touring. With the departure of Gillan and Glover, Blackmore was the only regular songwriter left in the band, but he soon encouraged Hughes and Coverdale to come up with ideas. Both spent time at Blackmore's Surrey home, working alongside him. Hughes had obviously written songs with Trapeze, but for Coverdale it was a completely new experience. In September the new MKIII line-up decamped to the splendour of Clearwell Castle in the Forest of Dean, Gloucestershire to continue writing and to rehearse new song ideas. At first Coverdale felt like a fish out of water, but it was an impressive place for him to celebrate his 22nd birthday on 22nd September as lead singer of Deep Purple. In particular the lavish living that was experienced in such a luxurious location was a complete revelation for someone who had just left his job as a boutique salesman in exchange for the bright lights. Coverdale was also surprised by the personal indulgences of his new, fellow band members: "Interestingly no drugs had surfaced and there had been no discussion about them. It appeared that 'booze' was the 'drug' of choice for the Deeps, well at that time, anyway," he recalled a couple of years ago.

The day after Coverdale's birthday the music press was invited to Clearwell for the unveiling of the new line-up. After a month at Clearwell, lots of new ideas were in place but before they could be recorded, Jon Lord had been commissioned to do another performance of his Gemini Suite, this time in Germany. Germany was far more receptive to this blending of rock and classical than UK audiences. Furthermore, apart from performing the 'Gemini Suite,' it also gave him the opportunity to premiere a new composition. Lord had hooked up with Eberhard Schöner, conductor of the Munich Chamber Opera Orchestra, with whom he jointly composed a new piece, 'Continuo On B.A.C.H', an interpretation of an unfinished Fugue by J.S Bach. The concert was staged at the Circus Krone in Munich on 4th October. New boy Glenn Hughes went along to share the vocal duties along with Purple Records signing Yvonne Elliman. The other rock musicians brought in for the event were Spencer Davis Group's drummer and guitarist, Pete York and Ray Fenwick, as well as Roxy Music's saxophonist Andy Mackay. As was the case with the "Concerto," the exposure of the event in Germany prompted German TV to commission Lord and Schöner to provide another new composition for the final gala night of Munich's four-day Prix Jeunesse festival for young composers in June '74.

October also saw Ian Gillan announcing the opening of his new recording studio. Gillan had bought the De Lane Lea Studio in Holborn before his departure from Purple and renamed it Kingsway. Meanwhile, following Lord's orchestral venture, Deep Purple reconvened in November to record the first album with Coverdale and Hughes. They chose to return to Montreux,

Switzerland, the scene of one of their most successful moments. This time the upheavals that had occurred with 'Machine Head' were thankfully non-existent. They continued in the Purple tradition of not using a conventional studio, and the modern conference centre proved an adequate venue, along with the Rolling Stones Mobile Unit and the band's trusty engineer Martin Birch. The music shifted towards the bluesier style that Blackmore had desired and was the architect of. Coverdale and Hughes fitted in well and the vocal harmonies also gave Purple a new sound. Another noticeable difference was Jon Lord's use of synthesizers. Contemporaries like Keith Emerson had been using synthesizers since the start of the seventies; Lord was slower to embrace the new technology, considering himself an organist first and foremost. He had started using synthesizers on stage at the tail end of MKII's existence, but now incorporated them into the new studio recordings.

The traditional Purple sound was evident with the title track 'Burn.' This was a perfect example of the group's rejuvenation. Blackmore came up with the riff, which Jon Lord soon pointed out was George Gershwin's 'Fascinating Rhythm!' Blackmore claimed it was purely coincidental and that he had not heard it before, but considering his musical knowledge and the fact that his 1965 solo single covered a Glenn Miller tune, it's more likely that the melody was subconsciously in his mind when he wrote it. Both Blackmore and Lord bristled with renewed energy and put in great solos, and Lord's use of synthesizers was evident and entwined perfectly with his excellent Hammond organ work; however, without doubt the star was Ian Paice. His drumming style was full of exuberance and reminiscent of a young lad let loose on a kit for the first time, but with the added years of skill and technique he had acquired, he spills out all over the track with fills at every opportunity. The twin vocal effect added a new dimension to the band's sound and it was apparent from the outset that this group had no intentions of resting on their laurels or the image of the previous line-up.

Epitomising the blues direction was the seven-minute 'Mistreated.' "It's very difficult within the blues frame to come out with something that's different and that's why I find it a challenge with the blues. It's a case of slowing down and playing three or four notes very well with a good vibrato, which is a lot more difficult than it seems on the surface," said Blackmore in 1983. Purple had always flirted with the blues, such as the slightly more up tempo blues, or rhythm & blues as it is better known, exemplified on tracks such as 'Lazy.' With 'Mistreated,' Blackmore showed that as a blues player he was equal to anyone and, although most people revered him for his ability to play fast, when slowing it down as he does on this track his understanding of the blues is clearly evident. The minimalist approach that so many other players often forget is the key to the song's quality. It is as much about what is left out as the actual notes played that make it such a great song. Coverdale's vocal sits perfectly over the music and he produced a superb, heartfelt performance. It

would be hard to imagine the previous line-up producing such music. Deep Purple had clearly changed, but fortunately they still had quality in abundance.

A notable difference was in the writing credits. Songs were no longer automatically credited to all five band members. This was a decision largely driven by Blackmore. Lord openly admitted to Circus magazine at the time that, "the major force in the group for the last couple of years has been Ritchie. It's been his energy that's got us through a lot of our personal problems." New boy David Coverdale was soon aware of the way things were arranged: "I could sense, even then, that they all deferred to Ritchie and most definitely didn't want to piss him off but, still, it was quite democratic, and everyone contributed to the development of the songs."

Having been off the road since June, it was now time for MKIII Deep Purple to take to the stage. Irrespective of the fact that they had just produced one of their best albums to date, and perhaps mindful that Coverdale was still largely inexperienced, a handful of relatively low-key dates in northern Europe were chosen as the debut arena for the young Yorkshireman. Image was vitally important to the band and Coverdale had admitted that his wasn't really befitting for someone fronting one of the biggest bands in the world. Before the album had even been made, the Purple organisation had sent him off to a Harley Street doctor who had prescribed the podgy vocalist with slimming pills. Recently Coverdale has gone on record saying that the pills made him "emotionally edgy, at times disoriented and certainly sleep deprived." As a result, even before the first gig, Coverdale had seriously questioned just exactly what he was doing fronting the mighty Deep Purple: "I didn't tell the band or management that in my chemically compromised state I'd considered leaving before I'd even done a show ... yes ... I'm glad I didn't go that far - very glad, indeed."

The tour was planned to start in Denmark's second city, Aarhus, but the plane arrived too late and 4,000 disappointed fans were told the news shortly before the gig was due to start. What was scheduled as the second gig therefore became Deep Purple MKIII's debut at the KB Hallen, in Copenhagen, Denmark on Saturday 8th December 1973. Despite Coverdale's nervous state he sailed through the gig with flying colours. By and large it was really only Deep Purple in name, with very little comparison with the MKII line-up. Of course the three original members were still the backbone of the group, but the new sound was vastly different. The deliberate decision taken to radically revamp the stage set effectively made comparison a futile gesture. Six of the eight numbers from 'Burn' were introduced, and only two older numbers were retained. 'Smoke On The Water' was now such a hugely popular tune globally that, had they not played it, Purple might well have been lynched. The only other MKII number was 'Space Truckin',' retained as the closing number of the main set. Regularly clocking in at thirty minutes, it was predominantly instrumental, but did add a section where Glenn Hughes could get a bit funky, something that would in time have a detrimental effect on the group's future. Opening the show with four new songs was a brave move, especially considering that the album had not even been released at this stage! For Purple to play a show comprising unfamiliar music shows just how much faith they had in the new songs.

Whilst in Denmark on the debut MKIII tour, the management was keen to get a new song recorded for a potential single b-side, rather than relying on one of the existing album tracks. Following the debut gig a studio was booked for the next day, but with the band having partied hard to celebrate the show, things didn't quite go to plan. The backing took longer to get together than they would ideally have liked, largely due to their fragile state, and they only had the studio booked for a few hours so time was against them. Coverdale turned up late as he slept off the excesses of the previous night but, apart from the time factor, Coverdale's voice wasn't in good shape. Although some lyrics had been written, the end result was that Coverdale and Hughes just added a few backing harmonies and the track, 'Coronarias Redig,' essentially ended up as an instrumental with Blackmore soloing freely over the backing.

Shows in Brussels and Frankfurt concluded the mini warm-up tour, and following the Christmas break a few more shows were played in France and Germany in January. The plans were to follow these gigs with a tour of the States commencing in February; however, Jon Lord had been suffering during the European gigs and was quickly diagnosed with acute appendicitis. The tour was put back and MKIII embarked on a month of touring in America in early March.

The 'Burn' album was released in February 1974 and proved to be far more successful than 'Who Do We Think We Are,' although with hindsight it is possible to say that it could have been even more successful had the band had its way over the choice of single from the album. With 'Smoke On The Water' being a massive hit in America, Warner Brothers were keen for a follow-up. Back in England, Purple had generally discarded the need for singles, having not released one since the relative failure of 'Never Before,' taken from 'Machine Head.' However, the band was keen to see 'Sail Away' as the single track. The revitalised MKIII line-up was obviously keen to create its own identity, and 'Sail Away' was indicative of the bluesier shift in direction that Blackmore had masterminded. The key to the song's strength is the marvellous groove the band creates. With a slightly funky rhythm it rolls on superbly, courtesy once again of Paice's effortless drumming style. Coverdale puts in a highly passionate performance, and with Blackmore's slightly funky playing, Lord's synth sounds and Glenn Hughes's singing and bass playing, it is Deep Purple a world away from the MKII sound, but equally as classy. Strangely though, with the exception of the album's one and only instrumental cut, 'A200,' 'Sail Away' was never played live.

Whatever views the band had about the song, Warner's considered 'Might Just Take Your Life' to have the greatest commercial potential. The song originated from Jon Lord: "'Might Just Take Your Life' came from a chord sequence of Jon's," said Ian Paice. It was inspired by the heavy organ sound of Garth Hudson from The Band's song 'Chest Fever.' As such, the song had very little in the way of prominent guitar, and when it was released in March '74 it was far less successful than 'Smoke On The Water' or even 'Never Before,' as it failed to make the charts in either the UK or US. Although we will never know if they would have had more success with 'Sail Away,' the band was at least proved right that 'Might Just Take Your Life' was not ideal single material. As most fans view 'Sail Away' as one of the forgotten gems from the Purple canon, the general consensus is that 'Sail Away' would have fared better, but such conjecture will have to be left as just that.

With Lord back to full fitness following his appendicitis operation, Deep Purple prepared for their next American tour in grand style. For the first time, and in order to make the long distance travelling around America more enjoyable, a private Boeing jet plane was hired for the tour's duration. For Coverdale, and also to some extent Hughes, travelling on such a grand scale was a true eye-opener. Sadly it also saw the start of drugs creeping into the band. Despite Coverdale's 'Cinderella' elevation from rags to riches in a matter of just a few months, it was the more experienced Glenn Hughes who pretty soon went off the rails. Although happy to have been elevated to the ranks of Purple, he soon became disillusioned with his role as

'second vocalist.' Although Hughes had impressed the band with both his vocal and bass playing abilities, he saw himself primarily as a vocalist. In fact towards the very end of his time with Trapeze, a fourth member had been brought in to play bass so that Hughes could concentrate on his vocal attributes. "The reality for me was that when I was in Deep Purple, I was so rich and so fucking famous and so unhappy because I wasn't really singing lead vocals, I was taking second seat, and I escaped into a world of drugs," was the way he explained it to the author several years ago.

The drug situation would deteriorate as time went on, but during the tour it was Blackmore's behaviour at the California Jam that was the major talking point. The California Jam would go down in history as one of the biggest gatherings of music lovers the world has ever seen. The venue was the Ontario Speedway stadium and the list of bands performing reads like a who's who of rock: Earth, Wind & Fire, Rare Earth, Black Oak Arkansas, Seals & Crofts, The Eagles, Black Sabbath, Emerson Lake & Palmer and Deep Purple. Official ticket sales were reported to be around 170,000, but some eye witnesses claim that, with the amount of people who found their way into the venue without paying, the total figure was nearer 400,000. Being such a prestigious event, ABC TV filmed it for a future broadcast, and although Purple was the headlining band they agreed that ELP would close the all-day event. The reason for this was simple: Purple had a gig the next day in Phoenix, Arizona, so getting off stage earlier would give the crew extra time to pack the gear down and prepare for the lengthy journey to the neighbouring state. Purple's contract stipulated that the band would take the stage at sundown, so they would be the first band on the bill to get the full effects of the stage lighting. To everyone's surprise, the event actually ran ahead of schedule and by the time the stage was set for Purple to go on it was still broad daylight. When the band pointed out that it was too early to take the stage, the festival organisers were less than happy and started threatening them, implying that if the band didn't comply they would never perform in America again. Being the most stubborn, Blackmore stood his ground and called their bluff. To ensure he had things his way, he locked himself away in his trailer, as Jon Lord recalls with some amusement: "Ritchie locked himself in his caravan, and they had sheriffs banging on the door and all sorts of American heaviness going down and our management running around like headless chickens, agents tearing hair. It was fascinating to watch and I'd love to see it all over again. It would make a great movie. To the eternal credit really of Ritchie it succeeded and we went on at sunset."

Blackmore explained to Cameron Crowe of Rolling Stone magazine how events unfolded: "The Who's producer - I won't name him - came into my dressing room and demanded that we go on immediately. I had just gotten there. I just ignored him. The guy kept standing there and said we'd be off the show if I wasn't onstage by the time he counted to thirty. I sat there, tuned my guitar and listened to him count out loud. He hadn't reached fifteen when I had him thrown out. Forget the money we stood to lose, it was a matter of principle. Even Jon Lord came to me in the end and said, 'Look, will you go on ... for the band?' I told him absolutely not and was ready to quit the band right then and there. Somebody else from ABC came in and asked me politely if I'd go onstage. I was angry, but because he was nice about it, I went on."

Eventually taking the stage just before sunset wasn't the last of the trouble; it merely set the scene for what was to follow. Blackmore always liked an explosive ending to a show when he knew the cameras were there, but no one expected him to put on quite the spectacle that he did as the show reached its finale. During the climactic ending to 'Space Truckin','

Blackmore had instructed his roadies to put some combustible fuel into the speaker cabinets, and at the appropriate moment they duly caught fire and exploded. But that was just the tip of the iceberg. During the guitar destruction, Blackmore decided to vent his anger at the organisers and focused on the onstage camera as a target for wreaking his revenge. Not only did he trash his guitar against the camera, but also rammed it into the lens, causing great distress to the cameraman in the process! "I hadn't planned to go for the camera, I was out to kill this guy who gave me the countdown. I thought he'd be onstage. If he had been, you would have seen more than a smashed camera. I don't like violence, but I was raving that night. He talked to us like we were absolute shit. Anyway, I couldn't spot him so I had a go at the camera," commented Blackmore in his typically uncompromising manner. With police, fire-chiefs and promoters all angered at Blackmore's antics, in order to avoid arrest he was whisked out of State via helicopter as soon as the show finished.

A year after the event he elaborated about the escapade in an interview with Steve Rosen, "It was in our contract that we were going on at 7 o'clock, I think. And it was about a quarter past six. And I really wasn't ready; none of my guitars were in tune. I had no clothes to wear; they were back at the hotel, where I'd left them. And I thought, 'Well, we're in no hurry to go onstage because we've three-quarters of an hour yet.' Then I was told if I'm not on the stage in thirty seconds, the whole show would be cancelled. And I said, 'Well, you fuck off.' There's lawyers fighting and managers fighting; it was quite funny."

The events at the California Jam certainly had a knock-on effect with the organisation, with Edwards and Coletta taking a back seat on the day-to-day affairs concerning the band's touring schedules. The escapades were getting too much for the managers and they handed over the day-to-day organising to crewmember Rob Cooksey. However, the age-old adage that "no publicity is bad publicity" certainly applied to the events surrounding this concert. "We definitely sold albums after that and got a great response around the world," said Hughes. Whether or not Blackmore's behaviour was on the spur of the moment or premeditated, he certainly knew how to draw attention to the band and Deep Purple's line-up changes had done no harm to its popularity.

The hugely successful American tour was immediately followed by MKIII's debut in the UK. Before the dates had been announced, fans were told that Purple would be playing the smaller venues on an extensive tour, which is exactly what they did. Blackmore explained, "we've insisted on this extensive tour. All our fans should have the opportunity to see the new line-up." Indeed there were no fewer than 23 dates covering Britain extensively, although Liverpool was omitted from the schedule causing some 'scouse' fans to plead via the music press for Purple's management to reconsider this omission; however, this fell on deaf ears. Having said this, in the early seventies the UK had very few large venues anyway! London's Wembley Empire Pool and Earl's Court were two of very few, but outside the capital the old cinemas and Victorian theatres were really all that was on offer. But even in London, although Purple could have played one large show, they opted instead to perform at three separate venues, undoubtedly much to the annoyance of the road crew. Following a gig in Stoke, the first of the dates in the Capital was at the Hammersmith Odeon on 9th May. Roger Glover was in attendance at this show and honestly expressed his views: "I didn't like it but I was probably prejudiced."

With the majority of venues being relatively small, this did result in some doubling up. Glasgow had sold out and a second show was added and, likewise, directly after Hammersmith two gigs were played at Norwich's Theatre Royal. Without a day off, it was then back to the Lewisham Odeon in South London for the second of the three performances in the Capital. Graham Hough, a film student at Leeds University, sought permission from Purple's management to film parts of the show as well as doing backstage interviews. With Blackmore having his own dressing room, the film crew had to wait until the Manchester gig to get their chat with Blackmore, but the whole event was a good indication of how different the business was back in the seventies. One could hardly imagine a top band of today allowing a film student such free access, but for Hough it clearly paid off as he ended up with a job at the BBC where he still works. Sadly, due to the prohibitive cost of celluloid Hough and his crew didn't film the entire show.

Once the film crew did catch up with Blackmore three nights later, his interview was full of the usual Blackmore wind-ups and dismissive comments, but it did throw up one hilarious comment. When questioned why he didn't share a dressing room with the rest of the band, he initially answered truthfully and straight-laced before going on to show the dry sense of humour he possesses, that is more often than not lost on most people: "I have my own dressing room because I like to tune up and I like my solitude before I go on stage. I tend not to get too involved in people because to be quite honest I find a lot of people boring. I find myself boring most of the time. I always like to be the opposite; I always was at school, that's why I don't smoke. I used to find everybody at school smoking, rebellious image, so because of that I won't smoke and never had. Mind you I was probably doing other things that were just as bad if not worse. I'm still very moody, shy and very honest which a lot of people can't take. The hardest thing in this business is sincerity. Once you can fake that you're laughing."

The third London gig was in the North of the city at the State Gaumont in Kilburn, and like Lewisham it too was recorded (albeit only on audio), this time professionally by the BBC for its 'In Concert' programme. As was quickly becoming a regular occurrence for Deep Purple, despite the fact that the audio document showed that the band was on top form, they declined to do an encore. It is thought that this was as a result of the band's disappointment with the crowd's lack of enthusiasm. Although it is feasible that the audience's reception was a reflection of their feelings towards the new line-up, according to those who were present it was simply a case of heavy-handed security pushing fans back into their seats every time they got excited!

As had been the case in America, Elf was the support band and by now they had been signed to Purple's own label, bonding them closer to the Purple organisation in the process. The second Elf album 'Carolina County Ball' had been released just prior to the tour, with Roger Glover handling the production. Elf Roadie Raymond D'addario recalls that, despite the growing bond between the two bands, Elf fell prey to Blackmore's love of practical jokes: "We used to play all these little theatres with orchestra pits and one of the last shows we did, Ritchie had the crew go out and get all these bags of flour and they put holes in them and pelted Elf with them. There was Ronnie trying to sing and these little bags of flour hit him and exploded."

Aside from a couple of isolated gigs, June and July were set aside for free time before the band returned to Clearwell Castle to start rehearsing for the next album. The free time was nothing more than a busman's holiday for Jon Lord, who completed two outside projects. 'First Of The Big Bands' was a joint collaboration with Tony Ashton that the pair had been working on sporadically over a couple of years. Although the sleeve information gave little away, it featured Cozy Powell and Terry Cox on drums, Howie Casey and Dave Caswell were among the horn players, and several guitarists were used: Peter Frampton, Mick Grabham, Caleb Quayle and Ronnie Wood.

"Ronnie had to leave halfway through the 'We're Gonna Make It' take," explained Lord to Melody Maker. "It's amazing to me that the album hangs together as well as it does, considering it was done over two years," continued Jon. "Actually there was one break of about ten months when no recording was done at all. This was at the time that Tony joined Family and Deep Purple were touring overseas."

The commission by German TV to perform at the final gala night of Munich's four-day Prix Jeunesse festival for young composers went ahead on 1st June. Not only did Lord and Schöner once again perform the 'Continuo On B.A.C.H' piece, but they also premiered a new work called 'Windows.' Although the evening was a success, Lord was less sure about the decision to release the recording, which Purple Records put out at the same time as the 'First Of The Big Bands' album. "'Windows' was never intended as an album, it was simply a concert in Munich. I'm not personally convinced at the moment that it makes best sense on an album," he said defensively. It was without doubt the most challenging of his orchestral works, and one gets the distinct feeling that Schöner's joint involvement was largely the reason behind this more disjointed and experimental work. Lord was honest enough to explain that he had reservations about it: "I was asked to do it in England but turned it down. Harlech TV were interested in putting it on at Caernarfon Castle and there was also talk of the Albert Hall. I must admit to having chickened out slightly. Although it worked in Germany I don't think it would work in England."

With Lord involved in side projects, even Ritchie Blackmore was roped in to do his first session for several years, for sixties star Adam Faith. However, when it was released most Purple fans were probably oblivious to it. In 1973, Faith had been seriously injured in a car crash, but not only did he miraculously survive he actually made a full recovery. Although his singing career had declined, he had tried his hand at acting in the popular UK TV series, 'Budgie.' Faith was also gaining success managing new singing sensation Leo Sayer, so his recording career was definitely playing second fiddle. However, he signed a deal with Warner Bros for a comeback album, appropriately called 'I Survive.' Faith wanted the introduction to the opening track ('I Survived') to simulate a car crash and specifically asked Ritchie to play the passage. "We were thinking who would be the perfect person for the piece and Ritchie was the one. What he's done is brilliant," explained Faith when he spoke to Melody Maker just after the album was released. The album was recorded at Kingsway with Martin Birch engineering. He also played rhythm guitar on the same track, and it is most likely that it was through Birch that Blackmore was brought into the session. Sadly the opening thirty seconds of the album was Blackmore's only contribution to the record, and it remains one of his most obscure sessions.

While Purple were enjoying this brief period of relative relaxation, Roger Glover announced to the press his ambitious new project. Despite the bitterness involved in being squeezed out of the band, he didn't walk away from the organisation that had effectively dispensed with his services as a member of Deep Purple. In August Glover spoke to Melody Maker, explaining what he had been doing since that last tour of Japan a year earlier: "When I left Deep Purple I took a job as A & R man with Purple Records. It didn't really agree with me though, and I felt a bit like I'd retired, and it's a thankless task having to listen to young hopefuls and turn them down." Glover had spent the rest of his time with outside production and session work. Within the Purple organisation he continued his involvement with Elf; outside of the Purple set-up he worked with Scottish band Nazareth for which he went on to produce three albums. Later he also went on to produce Rory Gallagher, Judas Priest

and Status Quo amongst others. But the main reason for speaking to the press was to promote what was undoubtedly the most demanding project he had involved himself with since leaving Purple. 'The Butterfly's Ball, and the Grasshopper's Feast,' a poem by William Roscoe from 1807, had been the inspiration for Alan Aldridge's picture book of the same name published in 1973 in conjunction with contemporary writer William Plomer. The book sold well and the inevitable spin offs ensued. Plans were in place for a 26 part TV series, a full-length animation for cinema, a stage musical and a soundtrack, and Glover was approached to write the music.

On the face of it, approaching a musician renowned for being in one of the heaviest bands in the world seems like an odd choice for a project aimed at an easy listening family audience. Glover seemed just as puzzled as anyone else as to why he was commissioned: "I still haven't a clue how it came my way. I had been in a well-known band where I helped to write a lot of songs, but why on earth they entrusted me with the project I'll never know." Glover's own theory is that the idea for him to do it came from British Lion Films. This company had been involved with the "Concerto" project back in 1969, and Glover met John Craig from the film company who offered him the work. Glover later heard that Pink Floyd were also in the running for the project. "Maybe they were looking for a heavy progressive band," said Glover. "The music at the moment is coming out fairly unheavy. None of it is heavy rock. I really don't like heavy rock," he explained, somewhat unexpectedly. "There's one song I'd like to make vicious and aggressive though, and for that I'd like to get Dave Coverdale." Although Glover had openly admitted he hadn't been impressed with the new line-up at the Hammersmith gig he attended, he didn't let his prejudice get in the way of recognising Coverdale's talent, although his desire to have Deep Purple's new singer perform on his own project must have seemed a little surprising to many people at the time. With Deep Purple MKIII due to go back on tour later in the year, Glover also expressed his feeling about no longer being in the band: "I've missed being on the road a lot more that I thought I would. When I left the band it was great to be off the road because it had been one long slog. The music wasn't alive anymore, the music was dead, and it was just going on stage and going through the motions. But what I miss now is hard to define. It's not hotels, planes, dressing rooms; it's that confrontation with the public. I don't get that anymore."

If 'Burn' had been in effect a debut album from a new band, at least it launched Deep Purple MKIII in grand style. Follow-ups are notoriously tricky albums to make, and 'Stormbringer,' the successor to 'Burn,' supports this theory. "We went down to Clearwell Castle for two weeks' very lax rehearsal, but that was as much of a rest as anything else," said Coverdale. "At most of the sessions only some members of the group were there." 'Stormbringer' was the first Purple album since 'Fireball' for which the band used the full and conventional studio set-up. The chosen venue was Musicland studios in the basement of the Arabella Hotel in Munich, but the way the album came together wasn't in quite the same easy, free-flowing way that 'Burn' had. "We went to Munich with very little worked out," said Coverdale. We had been working so hard promoting the new band and convincing people of its worth that we never had any time to write. When we were told it was time for a new album, we suddenly realised we'd forgotten all about it." Given Coverdale's comments to Melody Maker shortly after the album had been completed, it's quite astonishing to think that only a few months before there had been some suggestion that the album could have been a double record with each band member getting the chance to have a section for their own ideas. Such a concept wasn't new; in fact, Pink Floyd had done that very same thing with its 'Ummagumma' album in 1969. But as Floyd was a four-piece as opposed to Purple's quintet, it's not clear as to how two sides of vinyl would have been evenly shared!

The album saw the first loosening of Ritchie Blackmore's tight grip on the band. His marriage was in the process of breaking up and the personal problems in his life appeared to have a negative affect on his ability to write new material. "Ritchie might have been losing his grip a little. David and I were firmly implanted by '74," explains Hughes. "He didn't bring a lot of songs into 'Stormbringer,' I brought a lot more and he played brilliantly on the stuff I wrote, but probably midway through it he was thinking about leaving and of course we didn't have a clue about it." As Hughes explains, both he and Coverdale were now fully entrenched in the Deep Purple machine and were far more confident in bringing their ideas to the recording sessions. Both men's influences were also vastly different to Blackmore's, which were changing anyway. Aside from the personal problems, Glenn Hughes observed, "David and I listened to black artists from Kool & The Gang to Stevie Wonder to the Ohio Players and Sly & The Family Stone. Blackmore was going more Bach orientated." Indeed, Blackmore's growing interest in mediaeval, renaissance and baroque music were worlds apart from the cool, funky American sounds favoured by the others, as he has explained on several occasions: "1974 - that's when it hit me with David Munrow (leader of the Early English Music Consort). That's what set my mind thinking. But I used to love just listening to it - that was enough. Play rock 'n' roll. Listen to Renaissance music."

For the first time since 1969, Blackmore no longer had a writing credit on every song. Musical differences are nearly always cited when there are divisions within groups, but in this case it was absolutely true. While Hughes in particular was keen to explore his black music influences, or "shoeshine" music as Blackmore referred to it, Blackmore was more interested in learning to play the cello! With Blackmore taking a back seat in the creative process, the sound of Deep Purple changed quite significantly with 'Stormbringer.' There were still a couple of notable rockers penned by Blackmore – the title track and 'Lady Double Dealer' – but elsewhere on the record Glenn Hughes stamped his identity with the funkier, more soulful numbers such as 'Can't Do It Right,' 'Holy Man' and 'Hold On.' The last was a number that to this day Blackmore still hates. He claims to have recorded the solo in one take and by using only one finger, such was his disdain for the song. Given Blackmore's reputation for winding people up with tall stories, perhaps his claim should be taken with a pinch of salt given the quality of the performance. Either that or his talent is even greater than he has previously been credited with. But if Blackmore had played on the track reluctantly, the same attitude also applied with the ballad 'Soldier Of Fortune' that closed the album. Jointly composed by Blackmore and Coverdale, it was disliked intensely by the other three band members and Blackmore recalls that it was an uphill struggle just to get them to play on it. "Dave and I wrote that song. It's one of my favourite songs. It's got a few of those mediaeval chords. You will be surprised how difficult it was to convince the others to play that song. Jon fairly quickly said okay, but Ian and Glenn didn't want to know about it. So I said 'I'll play your funky song if you will play mine.' So he said as casually as possible: 'Okay I'll do it.' Glenn hated that song he thought it was shit. Ian quit after two takes as well. Not enough for him to do in that song to prove himself."

However, the major disagreement on the album saw Blackmore sidelined with his desire to do a cover tune. Such songs were commonplace on the first three albums, but once the band's song writing developed, covers became a thing of the past.

Blackmore was enamoured with 'Black Sheep Of The Family,' a personal favourite from Quatermass's one and only self-titled album from 1970. The song was first introduced to Blackmore shortly after Quatermass had recorded it. Blackmore's old pal, Quatermass drummer Mick Underwood, popped into the studio to see Ritchie during the making of 'In Rock' with the tape of their newly recorded song. Underwood played the song to Blackmore, who was clearly impressed with what he heard. It wasn't one of Quatermass's own compositions, but the song had been written by Steve Hammond who had been in Fat Mattress II, a group that was formed after the original version split from the band's founder, Noel Redding. The other members re-grouped with Steve Hammond effectively replacing Redding on guitar.

However, whatever the song's pedigree might have been, the rest of the band refused to do it and for the first time Ritchie Blackmore's ideas were being sidelined. It's still unclear as to whether or not the rest of the band just disliked the song or refused to do it simply because it hadn't come from within the group. Blackmore was in no doubt as to the reason why it was rejected. He put forward his theory to the author in 1998: "I put it to Purple: 'Let's do this song.' They said: 'No, why should we?' I'm like: 'Well, it's such a great song,' and they went: 'No, we didn't write it.' 'What's that got to do with it? Because you won't get any writing credits, you won't do this song?' 'Yes.' That was basically the bottom line. That threw me. If somebody comes along and has a good song, you go: 'Let's do that song,' you don't go: 'It's not one of our songs.' A lot of that went down with Purple, and I could never understand that. It was Paicey and Jon who were adamant about not doing anybody else's songs."

Jon Lord's version of events is somewhat different. Could it be that Lord and co. were simply annoyed that Blackmore was trying to introduce cover songs to the album, whilst at the same time holding his own ideas back? Jon Lord said: "During the making of Stormbringer he would play us something and say 'do you like this?' 'Yeah it's great, let's try that.' 'No, I'm keeping that for my solo album.'" In a classic chicken and egg situation, was Blackmore thinking about doing a solo album purely because the rest of the guys wouldn't record 'Black Sheep of the Family,' or had his mind already been made up? Of course, as far back as '71 he had talked of leaving Deep Purple to do his own thing, so at least for the time being there wasn't anything particularly devastating about Blackmore's comments. "I think probably through one of the songs like 'Holy Man' or 'You Can't Do It Right,' he was thinking it wasn't the kind of stuff he wanted to play. It was another band and was becoming something entirely new," explains Hughes.

'Stormbringer' was largely recorded in Munich, but for a few vocal overdubs done in August at the Record Plant in Los Angeles, where Martin Birch and Ian Paice mixed the album. At one point the album was going to be called 'Silence' and a sleeve design had been mocked up, showing a young woman

with her finger over her lips. Purple cashed in on its popularity and following completion of the album the guys went to Florida for the first of four large, outdoor stadium gigs. The other three shows were in Connecticut, Kansas and Texas, and in total the four gigs grossed in excess of £110,000, not bad for a week's work!

Aside from the internal disagreements that had arisen during the making of the album, other outside influences would also soon have an effect on the future of Deep Purple. The amount of money the band was now generating prompted accountant Bill Reid to instruct the band to move abroad or to accept the inevitable consequences of paying the vast majority of their earnings straight to the British Treasury. Under the then Labour Government, Chancellor Denis Healey imposed tax rates of over 90% for the very wealthy and the inevitable exodus followed with many businessmen and high earning entertainers setting up their homes and businesses offshore. Financially it made perfect sense, but there were knock-on effects for Deep Purple. Blackmore was the first to move to America, although tax burdens were only one reason. He also moved there in order to try and hold his marriage together and to follow his wife who had already set up home in the States. Jon Lord said: "It was disconcerting to some extent to be told you couldn't afford to live in your country of birth legally and there was this sort of wonderful way of getting round it. I actually didn't mind, I loved America, I was a great fan of America and we had toured there so much and I'd got to love it even more. We were told we could go and live in California and it would be wonderful. My first marriage fell victim to my move to America and a lot of other things fell victim to it as well."

For David Coverdale, just plucked from obscurity, the rags to riches story was potentially developing in to a 'rags to rags' story. "I'm just totally pissed off that people can be taxed so much. I don't know how much everybody in the band has amassed or how much I've got, but it bugs me on a personal level that the British Government can take so much. Before I joined the group I was getting £1.05 a week unemployment and I was supporting a girl and her baby on that. Now they have decided to tax me 98 per cent." All the individual band members chose to live in California, but it wasn't exactly a family gathering. Having been together for six years, Blackmore, Lord and Paice's familiarity with one another didn't necessarily breed contempt, but they certainly had become distanced from each other. The management team of Edwards and Coletta were also forced to move abroad for tax reasons, but while Coletta initially moved to California and Edwards to Italy, both soon ended up nearer to home in Paris. "We became isolated from the group. The only contact we had was the accountant who controlled everything," said Coletta. Day-to-day manager Rob Cooksey saw the decision to move abroad as a grave error: "The accountant wasn't aware of the practicalities of running a group. That was where things started to fall apart and the group resented that fact that John and Tony weren't there anymore." Glenn Hughes said: "The managers would fly to LA or Miami or wherever we were at and have meetings but it was all financial with the accountants."

Returning to the UK following their 'nice little earner' US stadium gigs, Jon Lord promoted his 'First Of The Big Bands' album with Tony Ashton with a live gig at London's Palladium on 15th September. Lord had told Melody Maker's Jeff Ward about the gig the previous month: "There will be a one-nighter featuring the Ashton Lord Big Band, with as many of the musicians on the album as possible. It'll be a twenty-four-piece band, which is rather exciting. We are going to rehearse for about ten days beforehand so that it's good. There won't be many heavy personalities; Ian Paice will be doing one of the drum spots and I'll be playing keyboards but I'm not sure there'll be any big names." While Lord was keen that the event was to stand on the merit of the music as opposed to the performers, he was also keen to make it a visual spectacle: "We'd like to use some of the effects and facilities they have at the Palladium; revolving stages, trap doors and all sorts of things." The show was recorded and broadcast by the BBC as part of its 'In Concert' radio programme, but as with the project with Eberhard Schöner, the music was vastly different to Deep Purple and was always only ever going to appeal to a minority audience.

Following this performance, a tour of Germany commenced on 18th September and concluded with a gig in Switzerland. Although the 'Stormbringer' album was still unreleased at the time, it was the first opportunity for most Germans to see and hear MKIII, and the same set list designed to promote 'Burn' continued to be used. However, if Blackmore's disillusionment with 'Stormbringer' pushed him into the background, he still appeared to be in control on stage. The same couldn't be said for events off stage, and rioting marred the opening night's gig in Bremen. The venue had a 4,000 capacity, but 12,000 fans turned up for the gig and the police had to use tear gas and water cannons to quell the violence that erupted.

In more peaceful circumstances, Roger Glover's 'Butterfly Ball' project reached fruition and was released in November. Glover wrote most of the material alone, although he co-wrote four tracks with former Spencer Davis Group keyboard player Eddie Hardin, and three with Elf's Ronnie Dio and Mickey Lee Soule. A host of musician friends were brought in to help with the recordings, which were done at Ian Gillan's new studio. Hardin actually did most of the keyboard work, although Glover himself tackled some piano and synthesizer throughout the album. A horde of guest vocalists included former Quatermass man John Gustafson, Tony Ashton, well known female session singers Liza Strike and Barry St John, and Glover's then girlfriend Judi Kuhl.

The most surprising choices were Deep Purple's replacements for Gillan and Glover, but there was no animosity as far as Glover was concerned: "They were in the new version of the band I'd just left and I thought they were good singers. It was nice to work with them." As Hughes had basically been brought into Deep Purple at Glover's expense, the latter's mature approach to the situation exemplified the dignity he had surrounded himself with following his departure. Hughes sung on the high pitched number 'Get Ready,' which helps to explain why Glover brought him in to the session: "The song was pitched very high and I had to have someone with a good range: Glenn was the obvious choice. I had no rancour at the fact that he had replaced me." Coverdale performed on a song called 'Behind The Smile' and as a pop tune, it showed another side of Coverdale's voice that Deep Purple's music rarely allowed to shine through.

The resulting album had a very easy listening, pop sound to it, which must have surprised many Purple fans. With Glover's image as a hard rock musician it was a difficult album to promote, particularly in the UK where, by and large, Purple had always been unfashionable with daytime radio. There was no array of digital or Internet stations in the early seventies, just BBC's Radio 1, with a very blinkered and inward approach to the popular music culture. Fortunately a more open-minded approach existed in the rest of Europe and the album sold very well, particularly in the Netherlands where it topped the charts. The single from the album, 'Love Is All,' featuring Ronnie Dio's vocals was also a big hit throughout Europe. It made the top ten in France along with a cover version by Sacha Distel that made the top ten at the same time! A short animation film was produced for this song, but the full-length animation project came to nothing largely due to a lack of finance.

Purple went back on the road in November for another American tour. Although the music was still of the highest quality, Deep Purple had clearly now had a very corporate existence. Observers noticed that the individual members had their own agendas. Hugh McDowell from the Electric Light Orchestra, who supported Deep Purple on some of the American dates in late '74, sometimes travelled in the private jet with the band. "I remember on the tour with Purple there was very little communication with them off stage. I flew quite a lot of times with them on the Starship. They all had their own seats, their favourite seats. The whole group had a very strong routine. I saw very little communication between the members at that stage. I think they were really quite bored with each other in a sense, going through the motions."

The excesses that tend to surround successful rock stars were also now having an effect on Deep Purple. Jon Lord in particular saw how the younger members of the band were affected by their sudden rise to superstardom, as he recalled: "Glenn being chased up the steps by a coke dealer with a gun, rushing to me saying, 'Jon have you got any money?' So here I am sitting on a private jet giving $2,000 to the bass player to pay off his coke dealer and they say it's all about music." Drugs were only a part of the problem and the tour saw the first inklings of a possible break-up. As well as the Electric Light Orchestra, once again Elf was included as support on a three-band bill. Blackmore's relationship with the band was developing and during the tour he took the opportunity of getting the band to help him out on a recording. With Purple having rejected 'Black Sheep Of The Family,' Blackmore was still determined to record the song and, following a show in Minnesota on 9th December, there was a break of a couple of days before the next gig. "I really wanted to do this song. I had wanted to do it for the last two years. So, I said to Ronnie – I got him around one night and I got him drunk

– 'Do you fancy doing it?' and he said, 'Yeah, I might sing it.' He got the song off in about half an hour. Then we went into the studio and we put it down. It sounded great except for some of the musicians involved who weren't really musicians."

Such was Blackmore's enthusiasm for the recording, and in particular the working relationship with Ronnie Dio, that a new song was also written and recorded. Blackmore said: "That was what started it. Once I heard that, I thought, 'Well, we're gonna need a B-side.' I just wanted to put it out as a single. No big deal. I just wanted to be involved in the song 'cause I loved the song so much. And we put a B-side down, which we wrote in a hotel when we were on tour. The song turned out so well, we didn't know which to put on the other side. So I thought, 'Well.' We were all thinking the same thing at the same time. 'When are we going to make an LP then?' So we said, 'Okay.'" The second session took place in Florida on 12th December. ELO's Hugh McDowell was also brought in for this recording, where they worked on the new song 'Sixteenth Century Greensleeves' that Blackmore and Dio had written together. As Dio explained, it came together extremely quickly: "Ritchie told me that we had to go into the studio in a couple of days to lay down a track, and asked me if I could write a lyric for him by the following day! We went up to his room and he played me the chords and I went away having to remember it. I went home and wrote the melody and lyric in my head, and it worked out fine."

"We were around the Florida area in Tampa. I remember he'd got these two-inch master multi-track tapes and Ronnie Dio came along. It was a day off on the tour and I put down some cello tracks. We spent a few hours there doing that," remembers McDowell. Blackmore's decision to use cello on the recording was an indication of how enamoured he was becoming with baroque music. Sadly these original recordings have never seen the light of day and, according to Blackmore, at least one of them didn't survive. The following year Blackmore spoke to Steve Rosen about his passion for the cello. "Hugh McDowell, he played on one of the tracks and is a good friend of mine, he is teaching me cello. I think unfortunately the track that he was on got wiped off because he was playing in America. But we have to do it again. He is brilliant and if I ever got a cellist in the band it would be him, if he was available. I used to watch him every night." The US tour concluded on 17th December, five days after the second recording session in Florida and plans were soon put in place to record an entire album, but the other members of Purple were not privy to Blackmore's activities.

As 1974 was drawing to a close, Deep Purple had the luxury of a lengthy break. The year had seen the band capitalise on the success of earlier line-ups. Press ads in The States proclaimed Purple as America's biggest selling album act according to the Billboard charts, although the figures actually reflected sales from the previous year and the bulk of Purple's success was as a result of the MKII line-up. Nevertheless, this hadn't stopped the band from having a hugely successful year on the road. The true mark of a group's success is its ability to capture the American market and Deep Purple at this time was as big a box office draw in the States as anyone. With the size of America, it's perfectly acceptable for a band to have a fair degree of success in just a handful of States and earn more than they ever would in Europe. Glenn Hughes's former band Trapeze was a perfect example of this – hugely popular in Texas and surrounding areas, but other parts of America were a different kettle of fish. Even when Purple had been struggling in America three years earlier when supporting the Faces, Rod Stewart's band only drew large crowds in certain areas. By 1974, Deep Purple's popularity spread from Florida to Washington, and New York to California, with all the stops in between.

As 1975 kicked off, Deep Purple had just one concert booked

at The Sunbury Music Festival in Australia. The festival was held on Australia Day weekend on a 620-acre private farm in Sunbury, Victoria. It has often been compared to America's Woodstock Festival, no doubt because of the venue chosen as opposed to the size of crowds that it drew. Farmer and local luminary George Duncan owned the 620-acre private farm on the southern outskirts of Sunbury, and the property was locally known in the district simply as 'Duncan's farm.' The concert was first staged in 1972, when up to 40,000 attended, up to 1975. Although it was not the first pop festival to be held in Australia, it benefited from the highest levels of promotion and publicity for any Australian festival and consistently attracted the largest crowds.

Originally starting only with Australian bands, by 1974 they had got Queen to play, who were apparently booed offstage by an audience that was more interested in seeing local star Billy Thorpe. The 1975 event that Purple was booked for would turn out to be the last time the festival was staged. Running from Saturday 24th to Monday 26th, Purple played on Sunday 25th. Although they were headlining, it was scheduled that local band AC/DC would close the day's bill. Accounts of what actually happened vary, but Deep Purple ran over the scheduled finish by around forty minutes and Purple's road crew apparently took ages to remove the equipment from the stage. Some claim that AC/DC got into scuffles with the Purple road crew, although what is clear is that AC/DC didn't get to play. Some reports state that AC/DC refused to play, claiming that the Deep Purple roadies provoked fights with them.

Who was to blame for AC/DC's non-appearance has never been fully explained, but David Coverdale recently talked about the event and recalled that, after a "less-than-satisfactory performance" to a dwindling, rain-sodden crowd, Deep Purple left only to hear more music coming from the stage: "Apparently, a young Aussie band had jumped onstage, plugged into our gear and started playing! Well, all hell broke loose, from what I was told. Our roadies (big buggers to a man) wrestled with the young band to get them off our equipment and off the stage. Chaos and frolics ensued. Of course, the band was a very young AC/DC. I cracked up when I heard – I thought it was great! And that is how I remember that episode. I worked with and got to know the lads many years later and we recalled that time over a pint or two. Very funny memory!"

Funny or not, one thing that is certain is that it was no laughing matter for the promoters. It had been agreed to pay Deep Purple something in the region of £40,000. For the promoters to try and cover the costs, the entry fee was A$20.00, rather expensive for 1975. It didn't help matters that the rain kept the size of the crowd down and, as a consequence of the bad weather, the attendance was reported to have only been about 15,000, well down on the previous years. While Deep Purple went home with its guaranteed A$60,000 fee, most local bands went home empty handed and AC/DC went home without even playing. The festival suffered huge financial losses and as a consequence this was to be the last of the Sunbury Festivals.

Several weeks of free time were available before Deep Purple kicked off its touring schedule in mid March, and Blackmore made great use of the time by recording his solo album. On 20th February he returned to Musicland Studios in Munich where 'Stormbringer' was made with the majority of Elf in tow. Elf had literally just come out of the studio, having recorded its third album 'Trying To Burn The Sun' at Ian Gillan's Kingsway Recorders, with Roger Glover once again producing. There were strong rumours at the time that Blackmore did some of the guitar work, but this was vehemently denied by all sides; Elf's guitarist Steve Edwards did all the guitar playing. Elf had also recruited an additional percussionist, Mark Nauseef, in

December '75, although neither was required for the Blackmore album. However, along with Elf's vocalist Ronnie Dio, fellow members Mickey Lee Soule on keyboards, drummer Gary Driscoll and bassist Craig Gruber all travelled to Munich for the sessions. Blackmore even used his then girlfriend, an opera singer called Shoshana, to add some backing vocals on a couple of tracks. Aside from the two songs originally worked up during the previous American tour, Blackmore and Dio jointly composed six new songs, with one other cover completing the album – an instrumental version of the Yardbirds' 'Still I'm Sad.' As with Purple's recordings, Martin Birch was employed as engineer and co-producer and an album's worth of new material was all written, recorded and completed by 14th March, just two days before the opening show on Purple's European tour in Belgrade. Having spent almost a month in Munich, it's astonishing to think that the rest of Deep Purple didn't know anything about Blackmore's activities. Ian Paice and David Coverdale had even arrived at the Munich hotel two days before recordings were completed, yet were oblivious to Blackmore's project. Considering that not only was Martin Birch involved, but that several members of Deep Purple's road crew – Ron Quinton, Baz Marshall, Willy Fyffe and Ian Broad – were also aware what was going on, it is even more remarkable that no one leaked the information to any of the other band members.

With the recordings completed, Blackmore, Coverdale and Paice headed off to Yugoslavia, where they would hitch up with Lord and Hughes. The two shows, one in the capital Belgrade and the other in Zagreb were the first time Deep Purple had travelled to an Eastern Bloc country. Pete Makowski, then a journalist with Sounds, was assigned the job of reporting on the unique appearance behind the Iron Curtain. Communist countries were renowned for their heavy-handed security measures and Makowski recalled how, during the second show, a girl in the audience tried to hand a note to Blackmore. Before she had the opportunity to do so a security guard pounced and punched her in the face. Blackmore returned the compliment with a swift kick into the back of the guard's head. Blackmore told Makowski after the show, "he was about to pull a gun on me. If he had tried anything the guitar would have gone through his head." Even this early in the tour, Makowski observed that Blackmore looked exhausted after the show. Was it the result of putting all his efforts into the show, or was he just physically and mentally tired of the whole Deep Purple thing? Blackmore said to Makowski, "See these hands? I probably own two fingers if I'm lucky. The rest belong to the management. All of my life I've been ripped off and undervalued and I'm just sick of it all."

Clearly this was a man coming to the end of the road with a band that he had driven along for the past eight years, a band that was arguably the best of its kind in the world and had reached heights few will ever experience; but self-satisfaction was clearly missing. The Yugoslavian shows were also treated as a warm-up before performances in Purple's more traditional territories, such as Scandinavia and Germany. At least that was the way Blackmore saw them: "I've got to admit I looked at those two sets as warm up gigs. I know it's the wrong attitude but I was feeling my way round – and the kids enjoyed themselves anyway." Furthermore, he had just finished recording an album that he was far happier with than 'Stormbringer,' and the writing partnership with Ronnie Dio was far more harmonious than the ego battles that Blackmore was caught up in with Deep Purple.

Away from the Eastern Bloc, the tour to promote 'Stormbringer' moved on to Denmark, Sweden and Germany. The set the band was now performing was largely the same as the one that they had introduced on the last American tour the previous year. 'Burn' was still retained as the opener, but 'Might Just Take Your Life' and 'Lay Down, Stay Down' were dropped and three songs from 'Stormbringer' were brought in to replace them: the title track, 'Lady Double Dealer' and 'The Gypsy.' Given Blackmore's general dissatisfaction with the album, it's no surprise that the three songs were those that included a major writing input by him, and this also showed that when it came to set-lists, the 'man in black' still had the say on what was played.

Deep Purple played the large Scandinavium hall in Gothenburg on 21st March. For Swedish fan Mikael Wiklund it was his first experience of 'serious' rock music: "This was indeed my first show with Deep Purple and the first show ever with a major band.

I started to listen to Deep Purple back in the early seventies and was completely hooked after I'd heard 'Made in Japan.'

I was disappointed when Gillan and Glover left the band, especially Ian Gillan because his voice was one of the trademarks of Deep Purple. A singer is very important for a group to stamp an identity, and these five people fitted together so perfect musically. Back to 21st March 1975, Friday evening in Gothenburg, and my first show with Deep Purple. The

expectations were very high. What songs will they play? How would they behave on stage? Will Blackmore smash the guitar? A Swedish support act, John Holm, started the evening with a 30-minute set. It was okay, but everyone in there was waiting for Deep Purple, and then, finally, the lights went down, and in complete darkness they entered the stage. What a feeling. Some flashes here and there in the dark from both cameras and that big mirror ball that they used to have hanging over their heads.

"They started to fool around on their instruments, still in the dark, and then Ian Paice gave us that well-known drum pattern and a wall of sound came towards us. It was loud! Finally, the lights went on and Blackmore started with the beautiful 'Burn' riff and off they went. Lord to the left, looking very cool; Hughes beside him, a lot of hair, Coverdale in the front, Paice behind him, working very hard, and to the right was Blackmore. Wow! 'Stormbringer' was next and after that, 'Mistreated.' That riff was fantastic to hear in 'full stereo.' The sound was thrown from one side to the other during 'Mistreated:' Very powerful.

Other highlights were, 'Smoke On The Water', which Ritchie started with the 'Lazy' riff. This was the first time that I'd heard 'Smoke On The Water' live so that was a very special feeling, 'The Gypsy' was fantastic live; 'You Fool No One', with 'The Mule' ending, ace; a very long 'Space Truckin'' where Coverdale sang some lyrics from 'Child In Time' and Ritchie played 'Hava Nagila.' Encores were 'Goin' Down' and 'Highway Star' and that was it! When it comes to how Ritchie Blackmore played and behaved and you compare this with other shows that I have seen, you can say that he was not that interested. His playing was, of course, very good, but he was kind of laid back, no energy."

Other eyewitnesses reported much the same as the tour progressed, claiming that Blackmore seemed disinterested and was not putting his heart and soul into the performances. It should therefore have come as no surprise when midway through the tour Blackmore told the management of his intention to quit. Concerned that it could have a negative affect on the rest of the gigs, the band was not informed of his decision; however, they soon sensed a change in atmosphere and, once Coverdale had confronted their manager who refused to comment, his suspicions were confirmed. "After we'd done a couple of gigs I began to feel strange vibes and I knew something was going on," Coverdale said to the NME. "I went to see Rob Cooksey and I could just tell from his eyes that he was keeping something from me. I could sense he didn't want to commit himself because Ritchie had told him something in private and he didn't want to break that confidence, even though it concerned us all business-wise."

With a brief break after the gig in Hamburg on 30th March, knowing that the remaining three gigs would be Blackmore's last, if not Deep Purple's, a swift decision was made to record them using the Rolling Stones Mobile Unit. The shows in Graz, Austria, Saarbrucken, Germany and Paris, France were thus all recorded with a view to releasing a double live album. It was probably undecided at this time whether or not the band would actually carry on, but just in case they didn't they could at least offer more products for the fans.

So it was that, on a pleasant spring evening in Paris, Deep Purple took to the stage for the last time with the MKIII line-up. Mike MacKechnie, a friend of the author, was present at this historic event: "I was on holiday with the family. Directly opposite our hotel was a record store that seemed to stay open for most of the night. I spent many evenings in the store listening to Tangerine Dream and attempting to hold meaningful discussions with various French longhairs, usually about the latest bits of vinyl to arrive, such as 'Physical Graffiti' and 'Stormbringer.' My 'O' Level French exam was still a year away, but I managed to bullshit my way into a discussion about the forthcoming Deep Purple gig, which I learnt was taking place at somewhere called the Palais Des Sports the following Monday.

"Armed with a flyer from the record store, I returned to the hotel with the ridiculous notion that for some reason my parents would let me, a fourteen year old, on my own and in a foreign country, travel half way across the city and back to go to a 'rock concert.' To my utter astonishment they said I could go - either my parents were more liberal than I had imagined or they had absolutely no idea what I was asking of them. I suspect a combination of the two. I made a practice journey on the French Metro the next Saturday to pick up a ticket from the Place D'Olympique. And at about 7:30 p.m. on Monday 7th April 1975 I wandered into the Palais Des Sports in my sta-press blue trousers (at least they were flared), Man Utd shirt and school shoes for my first ever gig. The first thing that hit me was the cigarette smoke – at least I think that's what it was, although I do recall a certain 'herbal' essence wafting around the cavernous hall. The second thing that hit me was the support band – this was fucking loud for my schoolboy ears! No matter, I discovered a way of resting my chin in my hands that enabled me to stick two fingers in my ears without making me look a complete dork (I had fashionably long, straight hair in those days, which concealed the heinous act).

I must admit I was a stranger to the concept of support bands (there was no 'plus guest' on the ticket), and for the first number I thought that Jon Lord had recently acquired a hideous perm and that David Coverdale didn't look anything like his photo in Melody Maker. It took a few numbers before it dawned on me that this was not actually Deep Purple, but somebody else – I never heard them mention their name and to this day I don't know who they were." (The band was Elf, of course.)

"After what had seemed ages, but had probably been

about thirty minutes, the familiar sounds of the Blackmore Stratocaster fired up amid a sea of dry ice, and the first-band-that-I'd-ever-seen-whose-name-I-knew laid into 'Burn' at a volume level even higher than before. Back went the fingers, and they stayed there for the entire gig. Other memories include a spirited rendition of 'Smoke On The Water,' with Coverdale singing in a deeper register than the Gillan version; a huge drum solo from Ian Paice, which I personally rank with the Bonham solo on 'Song Remains The Same;' an extremely long version of 'Space Truckin',' which finished the main set; and the pièce de resistance (well, we were in Paris), an encore (there I go again!) of 'Highway Star,' which climaxed with Ritchie smashing his guitar to pieces Pete Townsend-style. A nice way to finish the gig and, as I subsequently discovered the tour; and, as I discovered even later, the end of Blackmore's first stint in Purple. And that was that. I departed the hall with what felt like the bells of Notre Dame ringing in my ears, made my way with thousands of others to the nearest Metro station."

Although Deep Purple left an indelible mark on young fans such as MacKechnie, it looked to some as if Paris might be the last mark that Deep Purple would leave on the music scene. As the show finished, David Coverdale bade farewell to the audience and said, "We hope to see you again sometime in some shape or form," even though he knew that, with the last few notes that had just been wrung out of his Fender Stratocaster, Blackmore had just concluded seven years as Deep Purple's lead guitarist. Coverdale's comments clearly showed that he had visions of Deep Purple continuing. Would Jon Lord and Ian Paice, who twice before had gone through upheavals in the band, feel the same way?

- CHAPTER SIX -
WHEN THE DEEP PURPLE FALLS

FOLLOWING BLACKMORE'S departure, Deep Purple was now faced with the biggest challenge of its career. Lord and Paice were ready to throw the towel in, but internal pressure from Coverdale, Hughes and the management convinced them to find another guitarist and carry on exploiting the band's popularity. A few years later, Jon Lord openly admitted what the driving force was behind the decision to continue: "We were under pressure: the office, the record company, the publishing company. And surely there had to be somebody out there in this big world that could fit us well. We had always been a hard working band, because that was the way that we wanted it to be. When Ritchie left in 1975 we had been working like that for seven years, which is a long time."

Although the band was considering the possible options to replace Blackmore, clearly the management wasn't convinced the band would continue. HEC acted swiftly to keep the products being churned out while the remaining members pondered their future. '24 Carat Purple' was the first compilation of Deep Purple material released in the UK, and for many years it would serve as a great introduction to the band. Even though technically Purple was still a happening band, the compilation consisted solely of MKII material, suggesting that material from 'Burn' and 'Stormbringer' wasn't comparable. For UK fans who had missed out on the live version of 'Black Night' that had been released as a single b-side throughout Europe, it was included on the album, no doubt boosting sales at the same time. Elsewhere it contained a healthy chunk of MKII's finest material from the studio albums mixed with live cuts from 'Made In Japan.'

Coverdale soon put together a list of potential players. Top of it was Jeff Beck, second was Rory Gallagher. However, with neither Beck nor Gallagher interested in the role, the band auditioned several other players including Clem Clempson from Humble Pie. No one came close to the band's standards and, although Clempson impressed, his style was deemed not to fit their requirements. The third name that had been on Coverdale's shortlist was Tommy Bolin, but no one in the Purple camp seemed to have any idea how to contact the young American. UK rock fans would generally have scratched their heads when the name cropped up, but in America Bolin's name was much more familiar within the rock fraternity.

Thomas Richard Bolin was born in Sioux City, Iowa on 1st August 1951. Like most American kids of the day, his first musical influence was Elvis Presley. Although he was initially attracted to the drums, he soon moved to keyboards, then guitar and by the age of thirteen was playing in a band called The Miserlous. When Brad Miller, a guitarist with another schoolboy band Denny & The Triumphs, saw Bolin playing he suggested Bolin be brought in as lead guitarist. By 1965 the band had fired bassist Danny Foote and re-branded themselves as Patch Of Blue, performing a mixture of rock 'n' roll, R & B and pop hits of the day. Bobby Berge, who later played drums with Tommy in other bands as well as on Bolin's solo albums, recalled being impressed by the youngster, most notably for his work on a version of Tom Jones's 'It's Not Unusual:' "His solo really struck me. I remember thinking, 'hey, this kid is really good!'" Bolin continued with Patch Of Blue until mid '67 when he dropped out of High School and moved to Denver, Colorado, where he soon teamed up with vocalist Jeff Cook in a band called American Standard. But within a year he had moved on to Boulder City and formed Ethereal Zephyr, which quickly shortened its name by the removal of the first word. By mid '69 Zephyr secured a recording contract and released its self-titled debut album in October. A second album, 'Going Back To Colorado,' soon followed, but by early '71 Bolin and drummer Bobby Berge quit to form Energy.

Veering into jazz-rock territory, Energy proved to be a popular club act, although it failed to get a recording contract and folded in 1973. But Bolin's time with the band wasn't all in vain. Former Mahavishnu Orchestra drummer Billy Cobham employed Bolin to lay down the guitar work on his debut album 'Spectrum.' Bolin's astonishing work on the album brought him to the attention of a wider audience, not just in America but in the UK as well. Amongst those who praised his talent were none other than Ritchie Blackmore and David Coverdale, which prompted the latter to put Bolin's name down on his shortlist. Following this one-off session, Bolin then joined The James Gang, a band that had included Joe Walsh before he departed for a solo career, as well as joining The Eagles. Bolin was the replacement for Walsh's first replacement, Domenic Troiano, and cut two albums with The James Gang before quitting to focus on a solo career. A few other sessions took place, including one with Dr John that was never released, but Bolin soon upped sticks and moved to Los Angeles. He was laying down demos for his solo album when Deep Purple finally tracked him down just a few blocks away from where they were holed up, auditioning other guitarists.

Jon Lord remembered the initial impact that Bolin had upon him: "We were living in California and David had heard Tommy Bolin play and he said, 'He is amazing, unbelievable.' So we asked him to come over for a jam and he said, 'Yeah, I would love to man,' and he came over with coloured hair and things in it, and with this amazingly beautiful woman with him ... and

we all said, 'He's in the band!' She was so amazing, we all said, 'Can we borrow her for half an hour?' He played with us and it was great." For Bolin, he was torn between two options. Having achieved sufficient standing through his earlier work, he was ready to start recording his debut solo album; but at the same time, the chance to be in one of the biggest bands in the world was too good to ignore, although he openly admitted that he wasn't particularly familiar with Deep Purple's work: "I had seen them once on television in the States (The California Jam) and was very impressed. Besides that I only knew Smoke On The Water."

Once Bolin's appointment was confirmed, the press could at last be informed regarding all the speculation surrounding the band. It was announced in June that Blackmore had indeed departed, while announcing his replacement at the same time. Press statements also spoke about Blackmore's last three shows having been recorded and a double live album was expected before the end of the year. Perhaps wisely, given that they were more interested in promoting the new line-up, the album was put on hold.

When auditioning Bolin the rest of the guys immediately picked up on his enthusiasm and ability to jam. It was one aspect where Bolin was definitely similar to his predecessor. It was one of the factors that encouraged the group to take him on. However, one area where the two guitarists were clearly different was in character and personality. Blackmore was a dominant, intense, Svengali-like figure who wanted to be in control at all times and dictate his will to the others. Bolin in contrast was a laid-back, 'happy go lucky' character, and it was as much his infectious, light-hearted manner that endeared him to the group. Given his easygoing nature it is quite ironic that Bolin was given virtual control when the band went into the studio to record what would become 'Come Taste The Band.'

Filling the shoes of someone as popular and vital to Deep Purple as Blackmore would always prove to be a tough job, but Bolin's confidence was undoubtedly given a boost when Blackmore spoke with gracious praise for his successor. Blackmore spoke to Sounds just prior to Bolin entering the studio with Purple: "He's very good, he's one of the best. I think the band will probably be quite happy with him. He can handle a lot of stuff, including funk and jazz." But as always Blackmore appeared to have an uncanny knack of predicting the future, as was the case when he added, "maybe they'll turn into a rather different band, but I don't really think so. I think they know that if they did they'd be just another funk band. They'll still keep to the rock side of things, I'm sure of it. In fact the next album will probably be a lot rockier than 'Stormbringer.'" Blackmore's comments were also born out by Coverdale, as both men had gone on record as saying that 'Stormbringer' wasn't as 'rocky' as it should have been, and if Blackmore had stayed the follow up would surely have sounded more like the first Rainbow album.

With Bolin on board the band continued working at the Pirate Sound rehearsal facility in Los Angeles, jamming with the new guitarist and working out ideas for an album. However, with Bolin having signed a solo contract just prior to joining the band, his first commitment was to record material for his debut solo album 'Teaser.' Bolin assembled a host of fine musicians for the recordings, and even Phil Collins of Genesis contributed percussion on one track. He also wanted the guys from Purple to play on the album, but contractual reasons prevented this, although Glenn Hughes managed to sneak onto it, providing vocals for the last verse of 'Dreamer,' albeit un-credited.

Bolin was then free to reconvene with the rest of the band in Munich to start work on the Deep Purple album. As with 'Stormbringer,' the band once again chose to record at the Musicland studios, but for the first time in the band's career drugs really came to the fore during recording sessions, at least as far as Glenn Hughes was concerned: "'Come Taste The Band' was a drug-crazed trip in Germany," was the way he described it to the author in 1994. But even though Hughes might well have been 'out to lunch' for much of the recordings, Tommy Bolin was full of song ideas and certainly put a lot more rock into the album. However, the end result was a wildly different sound to anything the band had done with Blackmore. Bolin appeared just as confident in his ability as Blackmore was, and didn't seem concerned at all about filling such large shoes: "I suppose people will be looking for some of the things he used to do, but well, they are going to be disappointed. We play differently. I don't think he could have played what I played or what I wrote on the new album."

As a mark of Bolin's creativity, the guitarist was brimming with ideas and his enthusiasm for the album breathed new life into a band that had somewhat lost its way on the previous recording. Primarily by giving Bolin carte blanche, the band allowed themselves to produce an album that was radically different to anything they had ever produced with Blackmore. Jon Lord continued to take a back seat, thereby allowing Bolin a free rein. In doing so, Purple's major trademarks were by and large missing from the album. The end result was an album that was a much rockier affair than 'Stormbringer,' but to all intents and purposes it had little relevance to the name Deep Purple. That said it was still a great rock album. In reality, 'Come Taste The Band' was as much a Tommy Bolin album as a Deep Purple one and stands as a great testimony to his guitar and song writing talents.

The album kicked off in grand style with 'Comin' Home,' the new line-up's answer to 'Highway Star.' Although sounding a million miles away from the classic Purple of old, it still had the crucial ingredients of raw power, energy, excitement and fine musicianship. Bolin's presence is immediately apparent and his guitar solo, whilst hugely different in style to Blackmore, clearly showed the young guitarist had great talent. One of the most noticeable differences was Bolin's use of effect pedals and utilisation of different sounds, something that Blackmore by and large ignored. But the song didn't have a five-way involvement, as Glenn Hughes admitted years later: "I went home eighty per cent into the album. I'd completed most of my stuff but they recorded 'Comin' Home' without me because I had actually had a bit of a meltdown on the 18th floor of the Arabella Hotel, where I confronted a couple of my guys in the crew due to my intoxication behind cocaine." But if Hughes was having problems, things were generally looking good for Bolin at this stage. Not only had Blackmore praised him, but also the majority of reviewers agreed the album rocked more than 'Stormbringer' had and considered it a stronger effort by the band. Sadly this wasn't reflected in sales, and many Purple fans steadfastly refused to accept that the band had any life without Blackmore at the helm.

Bolin's time spent recording his solo album had neither restricted his ability to come up with song ideas, nor did it cause any friction within the band. Jon Lord was also working on solo material and, during the early months of the year, had scored another collection of pieces for a rock ensemble and orchestra. Following the completion of 'Come Taste The Band,' Lord took the opportunity to nip up the Autobahn to Oererckenschwick near Düsseldorf to record his own album. 'Sarabande' was recorded over four days with the Philharmonia Hungarica and a group of hand-picked rock musicians that included Spencer Davis Group drummer Pete York and session guitarist Andy Summers, who soon went on to world fame with The Police. The suite of compositions were all based on the Baroque style best exemplified by composers such as Bach.

Meanwhile the careers of Blackmore, Gillan and Glover were on the turn. Blackmore's album, recorded earlier in the year, was released just as Purple recorded 'Come Taste The Band.' Simply called 'Ritchie Blackmore's Rainbow,' Blackmore took great efforts to play it down as a solo album, but indicated that it was a new band project. Even though Blackmore was still signed to the Purple management, he wanted to make as clean a break as possible and for this reason he didn't want the album to be released on Purple Records. Edwards and Coletta set up a subsidiary label called Oyster purely for this purpose, and before long Blackmore also appointed Purple's US booking agent, Bruce Payne, to take over as manager and severed the connections further. Following his resignation in '73, Ian Gillan had opted to leave the music business entirely. He had grand visions of becoming a businessman, but Gillan was no more suited to business than Josef Stalin was to public relations, and his ventures into developing a motorcycle engine and running a hotel soon drained his finances to the point of bankruptcy. Eventually realising that his skills as a vocalist were where he was most likely to be successful, Gillan started working on a solo album for Purple Records in 1974, but it was shelved. The recordings did emerge on CD decades later under the title of 'Cherkazoo & Other Stories.'

Following Roger Glover's success with the 'Butterfly Ball' album, a stage performance was scheduled for 16th October at the Royal Albert Hall. The concert was a charity performance in aid of the Bud Flanagan's Leukaemia Fund and Action Research For Disabled Children. Glover used many of the musicians that had featured on the album, but not all were available. Ronnie Dio had sung the vocals on three songs on the album as the main character 'Froggy,' but now he was a part of Rainbow. Despite Blackmore having replaced the rest of the former Elf members in his band, Rainbow was preparing for its debut tour and, due to his commitment to Blackmore, Dio was unable to help Glover out with the concert. Glover decided to use several of the stage performers to perform 'Love Is All,' but for the other two 'Dio' songs he brought in Ian Gillan and former sixties model Twiggy! While Twiggy was given the song 'Homeward,' Gillan, who somewhat unexpectedly agreed to step in for the concert, had the job of singing 'Sitting In A Dream.' With Purple taking things easy before going back on the road in November, both Coverdale and Hughes also joined the stage cast, and even Jon Lord shared the keyboard duties with Eddie Hardin.

As a one-off spectacular the show was a lot of fun for the hordes of stars that took part. Even horror movie actor Vincent Price appeared as a narrator, linking the songs together. But for many it was Ian Gillan's appearance that was the highlight of the evening. It was his first stage appearance since leaving Deep Purple, and the rapturous response he got from the audience convinced him of just what he had been missing since quitting Purple two years earlier: "For me, horribly unfulfilled in my various business ventures, the show was one of great emotion, surprise and joy. I thought that with the passing of time and the on-going Purple I would be a forgotten star, yet at the announcement of my name for the song, the audience rose and gave me a standing ovation." The concert was also filmed, and to extend its shelf life further a cinematic production was produced. Film director Tony Klinger was given the raw concert footage, but in order to add some appeal to children the footage was interspersed with dreadful images of actors dressed in animal costumes. Glover recalls attending the première at London's Leicester Square and sinking further and further in his seat as the film rolled on.

The concert also included former Elf members Mark Nauseef and Mickey Lee Soule, as well as guitarist Ray Fenwick and bassist / vocalist John Gustafson, who had both appeared on

the 'Butterfly Ball' album. Soon after the gig, Gillan recruited Nauseef, Fenwick and Gustafson as he started putting a band together to re-enter the business. "It was Roger who brought me back with his 'Butterfly Ball.' Somebody dropped out and I stepped in. The reception I got at the Albert Hall was fantastic, so I went home and wrote a few songs. I had a great clearout after I went to live in Paris. I was still associated with the management of Purple, who'd upped sticks and moved to Paris. I took my band over there and we were rehearsing there for the best part of the year. I enjoyed it but nothing much happened so I came back and I'd neglected everything, so I decided to focus on the music again." Although Gillan originally used Mike Moran on keyboards, Mickey Lee Soule soon replaced him, and the Albert Hall concert was almost like a debut gig for what became the Ian Gillan Band. Despite the fact that Gillan owned his own Kingsway studio, the album was recorded at Musicland and was mixed at Mountain Studios in Montreux. Roger Glover assisted Gillan in re-establishing his career and produced the recordings, as well as supplying some instrumentation. While Fenwick, Nauseef and Gustafson had all been involved in previous projects with Deep Purple members, keyboard player Mike Moran soon became better known following his Eurovision hit single 'Rock Bottom' with Lynsey De Paul!

For Lord, Coverdale and Hughes, the 'Butterfly Ball' concert was a nice way to break them back into the live arena. By the time that Purple was ready to go back on the road with Blackmore's replacement, seven months had elapsed. Bearing this in mind, it is probably no surprise that they kicked off the world tour in Hawaii, away from the glaring eyes of the world's press. As with all previous line-up changes, the new one was faced with playing some of the older songs. As the group started rehearsing for the tour, the band had given Bolin cassettes of the earlier recordings to listen to and, whether or not it was self-confidence or arrogance, Bolin claimed not to have listened to the tapes: "I threw them away. I can do a few things like 'Smoke On The Water,' but didn't want to do things the way they were. I didn't even want to listen to those things because I thought it might influence me subconsciously." But despite Bolin's desire to do things his way, the other band members stressed the point that they wanted the guitar parts played closely to the way Blackmore had done them, which clearly wasn't to Bolin's liking. Before going on the road, Bolin was expecting a negative response from some fans, but responded by saying, "If anyone shouts, "Where's Ritchie?' I might just lean down and give the guy his address."

The set list was based around the new material and, unlike previous tours, there were several changes and variations as the tour developed. It was the first time that a Purple album had been so extensively plundered for a live set since 'Machine Head.' In fact, every track was given an airing at some point during the tour. Bolin also got to present some of his solo material such as 'The Grind' and 'Wild Dogs' from the recently recorded 'Teaser.' A few of the older numbers were also retained and the shows kicked off with 'Burn.' Inevitably, 'Smoke On The Water' had to be included; elsewhere, 'Lazy' was brought back in to the set, primarily to incorporate Paice's drum solo. 'Stormbringer' closed the main set and 'Highway Star' was reserved for the encores. For the first part of the world tour, Bolin was received reasonably well by the audiences, particularly in Australasia, and the six shows in New Zealand and Australia were a huge success. The band played two nights at the Festival Hall in Melbourne and Tommy Bolin also did an interview with 7HO radio after the first gig. Even though the show had gone down well, the interviewer asked Bolin to explain what happened when he had accidentally tripped David Coverdale, causing the lead vocalist's trousers to split! "The floor covering is like, linoleum. It was like ice-skating across the stage, you know... I'd slide over here, and there ... unfortunately, I slid and my right foot went out a bit too far, and he was walking backwards at the time. The lights went down, because it was the end of the tune; and when the lights came up he was lying on his back." With regards to Coverdale's trousers splitting, Bolin jokingly said, "He should go on a diet anyway."

This opening part of the world tour clearly showed that the band were good spirits. Before moving on to Japan, a slight detour was made to slot in a show in the Indonesian capital, Jakarta. This was a break from the usual type of country on the touring schedule, but the chance to make some extra money was too good for the Purple organisation to ignore. Had they known what was in store, it would undoubtedly have been bypassed. The Indonesian trip was marred by utter mayhem and the greatest tragedy in the band's history.

Firstly, Rob Cooksey had been told the gig would be in a 7,000 capacity theatre and the promoter sent an $11,000 deposit to show his commitment to the gig. In the end, this was all they got. Worse was to come. When they arrived in Jakarta, Cooksey discovered that the venue was a 125,000 capacity sports stadium, and that they had also booked a second show that the Purple entourage knew nothing about. The band played two shows at the outdoor Senyan Sports Stadium, Jakarta on 4th and 5th December, to an estimated 150,000 people over the two nights. The first concert saw around 20,000 people break down fences, but was relatively free of police reaction. "They let everybody be," said Jon Lord.

Back at the group's hotel after the opening concert, crewmember Patsy Collins, a well-loved celebrity of the British rock scene and Tommy Bolin's bodyguard, lost his life in a six-story fall down a service elevator shaft at the band's hotel. Following the gig, Cooksey estimated that there were around

100,000 in the audience, and calculated that two gigs on that scale should have grossed Deep Purple around $750,000. He demanded a meeting with the promoters, and although it started amicably enough, it soon turned into an argument, after which the two parties went their separate ways. Meanwhile, Patsy Collins evidently got into an argument with two other members of the road crew and left their room to go upstairs to his own. Peter Crescenti, who was covering the tour for Rolling Stone magazine, documented that: "The elevators in the hotel were operating slowly, so the impatient Collins decided to walk up the fire escape stairs to the next floor, only to find the door on the next landing locked. Then, inside the stairwell on the sixth floor he found an unmarked, unlocked door. He opened it and hastily stepped in, plunging three-floors down the service elevator shaft, crashing through some hot water pipes. The explosion was heard by another of the band's crew, who ran from the hotel lobby thinking a bomb had gone off. Boiling water cascaded through the lobby ceiling. A set of larger pipes had stopped Collins's fall, and though in shock, the stout, muscular man smashed through a door on the third floor, only to be trapped again by another locked door. Bleeding profusely and badly burned, Collins accidentally stumbled back into the shaft, falling three more floors to the main floor. Amazingly, Collins got to his feet again, found an open door and staggered into the hotel lobby, muttering, 'hospital.' He walked outside the hotel, climbed into a parked minibus and then collapsed. Hospitalised, he died early the next morning from internal injuries and burns."

Following the accident, the police arrested the two crewmembers Collins had argued with and later, the band's manager, Rob Cooksey. The three were held on suspicion of murder and isolated from the jail's other prisoners for two days, "with a kind of threat hanging over us," said Cooksey.

With three of their entourage in jail and one dead, Deep Purple played the second show the following night with approximately 6,000 armed and helmeted policemen, backed by dogs, circulating throughout the stadium. Before the concert began, an announcement warned any Europeans in the audience to congregate near the side of the auditorium. As soon as the show started, the rock-starved Indonesians were on their feet dancing. The police waded into the crowd, savagely butting, clubbing, punching and kicking the excited audience. The police then let the Doberman pinschers loose. Jon Lord later said, "Every time an effort to get up and boogie was made by any section, it was immediately pounded on." He also recalled seeing one mammoth dog dragging a kid across the floor by his arm, its teeth sinking into the boy's flesh. Frightened and sickened, the band played only half a set before leaving the stage. Over two hundred people were left seriously injured, and the crew and band were left deeply scarred by the experience.

Rob Cooksey was disgusted by the police behaviour: "All the time we were under suspicion of murder, they were making us sign autographs and things. You just wouldn't believe the mentality. They're all on the take, on the make." After interviewing two girls who were eyewitnesses to Collins's death, the police became convinced that it was in fact an accident and the three were released. Although Bolin believed that Collins had simply misread a sign, Lord was far more suspicious and to this day remains unconvinced that Collins's death had been an accident. "Obviously the guys who were arrested had nothing to do with it, but I don't personally believe that Patsy would step into a lift shaft. You don't open a door and step into the darkness." However, Glenn Hughes told one journalist a couple of months after the event that the story as reported in Rolling Stone was inaccurate: "We told them what to write, but that thing about him being killed was bullshit. I was the last one to see him. I was with him thirty seconds before he fell down the (elevator) shaft, and there was no one else around. He was really drunk." With Hughes's own perilous condition at the time, onlookers are surprised that he was able to remember much at all about those heady days.

Further problems continued to crop up for the band. While in Jakarta, Tommy Bolin's drug dependency also started to cause problems. Glenn Hughes recalled that Bolin took some liquid methadone and then fell asleep, lying on his arm. When he awoke his arm was virtually paralysed and Bolin was only able to play rudimentary bar chords during the second night's performance. Deep Purple's next gigs were in Japan, where the band was treated like gods, but Bolin's arm was still not fully recovered. When Purple took Bolin on, they had no idea about his drug habit. It was only as they went on the road that it came to the fore. Jon Lord said: "We didn't know that he had problems and how could we have known? And that was the sad ending of the whole thing. I mean, he was so talented, he could be brilliant. Some nights he could stand there below the spotlight and he could be amazing, a wonderful run could come from nowhere. He was an active person, young, good looking. It could have worked, had it not been for the problem with the arm."

Even though the band were unable to fire on all cylinders, Warner Brothers in Japan was always keen to get a live document, and with the previous line-up not having toured the country, they elected to try and repeat the successful formula of 'Made In Japan' three years earlier. They took full advantage of the opportunity to record the last show of the tour at Tokyo's massive Budokan Hall on 15th December 1975, but by now the Deep Purple that was performing was a world apart from the band that had produced one of the defining live albums in rock history.

After a break for Christmas, a lengthy two-month American tour did show some improvements from the experiences in Indonesia and Japan. Tommy Bolin seemed particularly upbeat about the situation. Even Blackmore and his new band Rainbow went to see the band perform. "Ritchie, you know, he's come and listened to the band, and he really likes it a lot, which makes me happy," said Bolin. The happiness didn't last long and, although there were some good performances on the tour, both Bolin's and Hughes's performances were erratic. Audiences didn't always take to the new look Deep Purple and Bolin soon tired of trying to replicate the songs the way Blackmore had done them: "At first there was a kind of restricted feeling around the group ... like, 'here's how Ritchie played it, play it kinda like Ritchie played it.' But that only lasted a while and now I don't care how Ritchie played ... I'm being sued by him so why should I care." Blackmore's legal team named Bolin as a correspondent in Blackmore's divorce suit against his wife, Babs. Bolin responded by saying: "I was in a drunken stupor for four days and I passed out at her place. She was always having these parties. I never fucked her or nothing." But if his problems outside of the music industry were briefly overcome, the audiences continued to give the new Purple a lukewarm reception.

The final major test was when Purple completed the tour back in Britain. The UK press that attended the band's brace of gigs at Wembley's Empire Pool (now called the arena) slated Purple's performances. One described it as a "huge cacophonous row." During the short, final UK tour Bolin was still sufficiently positive to tell one journalist about the band's future, "The new Purple album will be more experimental. Although I would think at the same time that this will be the last Purple band." The final part of his statement would prove to be far more accurate than the first.

Although there had been discussion about making a new album during the British tour, Coverdale, Lord and Paice were having serious reservations about their immediate future. "We went round the world with him, unravelling Deep Purple's reputation wherever we went. It really wasn't happening. Glenn was singing more and more like Stevie Wonder every day. Tommy was forgetting arrangements and bumbling round the stage, smiling a lot," Lord was to admit openly several years later. As Lord, Paice and Coverdale left the stage on the last night of the tour at Liverpool's Empire Theatre on 15th March, they had all had enough, and decided the band couldn't carry on any longer. Bolin would be proved wrong about another album but, like Blackmore, he appeared to be able to predict some things, as MKIV was to be the last line-up – well, at least for the next eight years – and Deep Purple folded at the end of that ignominious UK tour.

Glenn Hughes, like Bolin, was by now also heavily dependent on drugs and admitted in recent years that it wasn't exactly a bundle of laughs: "All of the band was dabbling in intoxication, whether it be drink or drugs. It affected my attitude for sure. I was very over the top in a lot of things. I'm not going to tell you that we had a great time, Tommy and I, cavorting around the globe stoned, because it wasn't great. But there were other issues that broke the band up." For a band that had scaled heights none of the musicians could ever have imagined, it was a shame that the band eventually folded, arguably for non-musical reasons.

Although technically that last night in Liverpool signalled the end for the band, the announcement wasn't made to the press until July. Just prior to this, Coverdale, Hughes and Lord all contributed to an all-star line-up album, 'Wizard's Convention,' written and recorded by ex-Spencer Davis Group keyboard player Eddie Hardin at Ian Gillan's Kingsway studio. The album also included Hardin's former band mates drummer Pete York and guitarist Ray Fenwick, as well as Tony Ashton and drummers Ric Lee of Ten Years After and Les Binks, who less than a year later joined Judas Priest. Roger Glover even turned up to play bass on one track, but anyone expecting something akin to Deep Purple would have been disappointed. The album was largely middle of the road pop and, when it was released in December, largely sank without a trace.

Although some would go on to argue that without Blackmore Deep Purple was always doomed to fail, the first rehearsals done with Tommy Bolin in California in the summer of '75 were captured on tape and officially released under the title of 'Days May Come And Days May Go' in 2000. Although the sound was a world apart from the Blackmore-fuelled band, these recordings do show that the potential was there. If drugs hadn't entered into Deep Purple's world, perhaps the band could have kept things on an even keel, even if it was only for one more album. But such suppositions will always remain as just that.

- CHAPTER SEVEN -
OVER SLEEPY GARDEN WALLS (THE AFTERMATH)

AFTER THE band's demise, Tommy Bolin focused on the solo career that he had put on temporary hold while he had toured the world with Deep Purple. He soon got a band together to promote the 'Teaser' album and toured America two months after Purple's last show. Ironically, this featured Mark Stein, keyboard player with Vanilla Fudge, the band that had originally inspired Deep Purple back in 1968. Bolin also became a lot more forthcoming about having stepped into Blackmore's shoes: "The first gigs were the best. They got progressively worse." By the time the group hit the states "it was not much fun anymore, and if you're not having fun it's not worth doing." In hindsight, Bolin shared the views of many others who questioned Deep Purple's decision to carry on after Blackmore quit. "They didn't need to do it, they didn't need the money and talent-wise they could do anything," said Bolin. "It was difficult following a guy like Ritchie Blackmore. When someone is the focal point of a group like he was, it's very hard to replace them. After a while it just got pointless."

After the successful tour, Bolin produced a second solo album, the superb 'Private Eyes,' and spent the rest of 1976 touring the States. He also expressed his feelings about the way he saw that Deep Purple had treated him: "A lot of things just got distorted, like stories about each other. After the tour they never called and we never talked. I don't know, but I believe a band should be a band. But I think Purple became frustrated and wanted to do more 'Smoke On The Water'-type, straight-ahead, kill-their ears, beat-'em-to-death music. 'Teaser' also got much more airplay than 'Come Taste The Band,' and I had to do interviews for that and for Deep Purple too, because the others were kind of 'anti-interviewish.'" Jon Lord and Ian Paice now had their own group and Glenn, after a one-off tour UK tour with his old band Trapeze, was mixing a two-record set of solo material and "laying back in LA, going out with Linda Blair!"

Hindsight is indeed a wonderful thing, and with it Jon Lord commented: "I was shocked and stunned that anybody would really think that replacing Blackmore was an option. However, I went along with it so someone must have said something to convince me. It was certainly nothing to do with money; we had plenty of money by that time. More than any young chaps of our age could have any right to expect. Then I met Tommy Bolin who was a delightful man, an absolutely charming chap. I was very taken with him and agreed to carry on. In retrospect I don't think it did Tommy any good whatsoever. I think he died as a result of it."

Fellow founding member Ian Paice in recent years he has gone on record in recent years as saying, "what should have happened was, when Ritchie said he wanted to quit, we should have said, 'Let's just stop and look at this.' He, Jon and I should have sat down and said, 'Look, if it's because of Glenn Hughes and David Coverdale and what they're doing, then let's change the band again or let's just take two years off. We'll all do what we want, come back in two years' time and look at it again.' That's what we should have done, because if we had, it would have continued through to now, and we'd have had a lot of fun all along. We would have done a tour every two years, made a record and still had a nice social circle. But when Ritchie left, we were a bit silly. We were determined to carry on and we brought Tommy Bolin in. As good a player as he was in the studio, he was hopeless on stage. When he got on a big stage, he

just seemed to freeze up. Instead of playing a solo, he'd end up shouting at the audience and arguing with them. Plus there were his personal problems which didn't help at all. That's when it became too much."

But Paice has also gone further with his assessment: "The last year was not fun at all. It was pure fun until Gillan left because he was very funny on the road in those times. You never knew what he was going to do next. You never knew if Ritchie was going to turn up. It was just very exciting. On the night something went wrong, it was terrible, but when you look back on it months later, it's hilarious. That was good. From the time David and Glenn joined it wasn't the same. The fun had left."

The Tommy Bolin band's last show of 1976 was supporting Jeff Beck in Miami on 3rd December and the group received a rapturous response. After the gig, Bolin posed for photos with Beck then, along with his girlfriend, he returned to his room at the Newport Hotel. Later in the evening he passed out, but came round again. Around seven the following morning his girlfriend noticed his pulse was very low and called for an ambulance. Unfortunately, Tommy Bolin died before he reached the hospital. The cause of death was later identified as multiple drug intoxication; he was just twenty-five years old. The news filtered around the music scene and four days later Ritchie Blackmore's Rainbow, on tour in Japan, dedicated a song to him.

Glenn Hughes had been the closest to Bolin within the Purple camp and they certainly hit it off musically. In 1994 Hughes told the author how he felt when he heard of Bolin's death: "He and I got on famously but we were sick though. We both had the same views on music and life. We stretched boundaries; we really were out there musically. But Tommy and I were sick; we weren't good bedfellows we shouldn't have been together. When he passed away it didn't really stop me from using unfortunately." Prior to Bolin's death, the pair had discussed the possibility of continuing to work together, as Hughes explains: "We hadn't actually done anything but we did some tapes at my house just fucking around." Hughes went on to produce his debut solo album 'Play Me Out' the following year but, from then on, his career drifted for many years from one short-lived project to the next while he struggled to deal with his cocaine addiction. These projects included collaborations with notable guitarists Pat Thrall, Gary Moore and Tony Iommi: The last, although intended as a solo project, was marketed under the Black Sabbath banner. Having straightened himself out in the mid-nineties, Hughes has spent the last decade re-establishing his career with a highly prolific output, including a collaboration with Red Hot Chilli Peppers' drummer Chad Smith on his most recent album 'Music For The Devine.'

David Coverdale soon picked up the pieces following Purple's demise and, having moved to Germany where he chose exile for tax reasons, started writing songs for his first solo album. He teamed up with ex-Juicy Lucy and Snafu guitarist Micky Moody, an old friend from his days in the North East of England. Moody co-wrote many of the songs and Roger Glover was brought in to produce the album. 'White Snake' was released in early '77 and Coverdale wasted no time in following it up with a second, stronger release, 'Northwinds.' By 1978, he had formed a band along with Moody, using the name of the first solo album, and his career continued to blossom through the eighties and beyond. He put Whitesnake on hold for a while and teamed up with Led Zeppelin guitarist Jimmy Page for a one-off album in 1993, before reactivating Whitesnake off and on with various line-ups ever since.

Jon Lord's solo album 'Sarabande' was finally released in October '76. It was far and away his most accomplished solo project and blended the rock musicians and orchestra far more successfully than his earlier works. But, despite being his most mature and cohesive album to date, its classical-based style was largely ignored by both Deep Purple and rock fans in general. Along with Paice, Jon Lord had remained the only consistent factor through Deep Purple's eight-year career, and the pair then put a band together with their old pal (pun definitely intended!) Tony Ashton to form Paice Ashton Lord, or PAL as it was generally referred to. Incorporating a brass section and female backing vocalists they produced the underrated album, 'Malice In Wonderland.'

When the UK tour was over, Jon Lord and Tony Ashton went over to the States to promote the album via radio interviews, before the band would meet again in Germany to start work on the second album. Although it was 75% complete, the enthusiasm had gone from the band; the sound was still there, but they had more work to do if they were ever to make PAL a huge success. With some superb guitar solo work on Steamroller Blues (a live favourite) and backing vocals by Bernie, most of the second album was done. However, Jon Lord and Tony

Ashton spent some time together on a Swiss skiing holiday during the Christmas of 1977 and decided that it was best to fold the band.

Following a brief UK tour, PAL started work on a second album, but Ashton was uncomfortable with his position of front man. Due to his heavy drinking some of the gigs had been less than spectacular and he even fell into the orchestra pit at the Rainbow Theatre in London! Paice admitted, "we took him out of his area of expertise and tried to make him something he wasn't. It wasn't his fault." PAL's style of music was also too unlike Deep Purple for most fans to comprehend, and the group disbanded before the second album was finished. After a brief stint backing Maggie Bell, Lord soon joined Coverdale in Whitesnake and a year later Ian Paice followed suit. This started rumours of a Deep Purple reunion. In fact, even within a year of the band's demise, journalists had already suggested that Deep Purple might get back together. Of course with Bolin deceased, any reunion would have to involve Blackmore, who by now had fully established Rainbow and was more than happy being top dog and in full control of his musical direction.

Deep Purple's name was never far from people's lips. The band may not have existed anymore but it was still a huge money earner. Within a few months of the demise, EMI had released 'Made In Europe,' a live album compiled from recordings of the last three gigs Blackmore had done with the band in April '75. Although the album didn't indicate exactly which tracks came from where, the bulk of it was recorded at the Saarbrücken show and only Blackmore's guitar solo came from the very last gig in Paris. Nevertheless, Martin Birch produced an album that, while it could never be considered as good as 'Made In Japan,' still showed that Deep Purple MKIII was more than capable of continuing Purple's reputation as a leading light in the field of hard rock music. Following Bolin's death in December '76, Warners in Japan also decided to release the 'Last Concert In Japan' from that fateful tour a year earlier. As with 'Made In Japan,' the original intention was to make a recording uniquely for the Japanese market. However, unlike 'Made In Japan' where the band decided the recordings were so good they should be released worldwide, none of the surviving ex-members were happy with the recording and restricted its release. Although import copies found their way into stores, it was never officially released in the UK or US. The show was also filmed and, as with Glover's 'Butterfly Ball' concert, Tony Klinger was involved. A twenty-five minute film entitled 'Deep Purple Rises Over Japan' was produced and it was screened on German TV in the early eighties. There was also a plan to release it on video in 1985, but the release was cancelled despite press adverts.

Further albums continued to be released over the ensuing years. For the diehard fans, previously unreleased concerts whetted the appetite: albums such as 'In Concert,' which brought together two performances recorded for BBC radio in 1970 and '72, and 'Live In London,' a 1974 live recording from the MKIII line-up, also originally recorded for BBC Radio. For the more casual rock fan, compilations were churned out on a regular basis. One of these, 'Deepest Purple,' reached number one in the UK album charts in 1980, proving how popular Deep Purple still was.

By now Ritchie Blackmore's Rainbow had departed with original singer Ronnie James Dio and embarked on a more commercial path that saw hit singles in the shape of 'Since You Been Gone' and 'All Night Long.' Rainbow's commercial success was largely due to Blackmore's appointment of Roger Glover to the ranks. Rainbow's manager Bruce Payne also managed Glover, so the bassist was fully aware of Rainbow's career. Given that it was Blackmore who had instigated Glover's departure, it looked to many as if this was an admission that he had made a mistake back in '73. Since then, Glover's career had predominantly centred on production work, although he had also helped to kick-start Ian Gillan's solo career. Aside from his 'Butterfly Ball' album released in '74, a second solo work came out a few months before Blackmore recruited him to Rainbow. 'Elements' was a far cry from either Deep Purple or the poppy 'Butterfly Ball.' It contained four lengthy and predominantly instrumental pieces performed by the Munich Philharmonic Orchestra with a few choice rock musicians, and was more akin to Mike Oldfield's early work than anything else.

The Ian Gillan Band that was assembled shortly after the 'Butterfly Ball' concert were all highly respected musicians and Ian Gillan had given them free rein to take the music anyway they liked. The jazz-rock style they indulged in wasn't to the liking of his old Purple fans and, after three albums, the group was disbanded and a new band simply called Gillan steered the vocalist back onto a rock 'n' roll path. Like Rainbow, Gillan soon became regulars on the BBC's 'Top Of The Pops' and

had three highly successful years with sold out concerts and top twenty albums and singles, before an unexpected move saw Ian Gillan join Black Sabbath in 1983. This only lasted a year. Not to be outdone, Whitesnake also started to attain a greater degree of commercial success around the same time and their first top twenty hit, 'Fool For Your Loving,' sat nicely in the charts alongside Rainbow. Although overall sales didn't eclipse Purple, Rainbow, Gillan and Whitesnake each had more singles chart success, proof if it was needed that the Purple style of music was still resonating with rock fans a decade on.

Deep Purple's erstwhile engineer and producer Martin Birch continued to work alongside the various ex-members. He produced the first four Rainbow albums, as well as Paice Ashton & Lord's 'Malice In Wonderland' and Roger Glover's 'Elements.' He was also involved with Whitesnake's career up to and including the 1982 release 'Saint & Sinners' – producing seven albums all told, including the band's live releases. He also worked with Black Sabbath and later had huge success with Iron Maiden, after which he retired as a wealthy man in the early nineties and has exchanged his engineer's equipment for a set of golf clubs! Sadly, despite the glut of unreleased recordings and original albums that have been re-mastered since the mid-nineties, Birch couldn't be enticed to oversee what were, in most cases, as much his babies as they were the band's, although he did contribute to the fabulous film made for DVD that charted the making of the 'Machine Head' album.

For original members Rod Evans and Nick Simper, unceremoniously dumped in the summer of '69, life hasn't been so kind. Initially Simper took a job backing Marsha Hunt, but by 1970 he had set up his own band called Warhorse and signed a deal with Vertigo Records. The band released two albums: 'Warhorse' in 1970 and 'Red Sea' in 1972. Nick Simper was particularly bitter about his departure from Purple and sued for wrongful dismissal. Simper, by then with a young family, accepted an out of court settlement in 1972 that gave him a one-off payment in exchange for waiving future royalties. By '74 Warhorse had come to the end of its contract with Vertigo and was struggling financially. Warner Brothers looked as if they would sign the band and paid for two demo recordings to be made, but eventually chose to sign the Heavy Metal Kids instead, and Warhorse crashed to an ignominious end when the PA packed up at their last gig. After attempting a couple of numbers, they had to call a premature end to the band. Along with Warhorse guitarist Pete Parks, Simper created a band called Dynamite, but this only released one single, and eventually the pair established Fandango in 1979 and produced two albums, 'Slipstreaming' and 'Future Times,' and one single, the Russ Ballard composition 'Wish I'd Never Woke Up,' before calling a halt on this band. Simper and Parks continue gigging to this day with The Good Old Boys, initially started with former Savages drummer Carlo Little, but now including ex-Strawbs sticks man Richard Hudson.

Rod Evans appeared to accept his departure a little easier and agreed to continue to receive royalties. Given the success Deep Purple achieved in the seventies, this was a wise decision. Having settled in America after his sacking, Evans produced a solo single for Capitol Records called 'It's Hard To Be Without You' that died the proverbial death and is one of the rarest recordings by any Purple member. In fact, the only copies that have emerged are promos and it is still unclear if the single was actually released commercially. Evans then joined a band being created by ex-Iron Butterfly members Larry 'Rhino' Reinhardt and Lee Dorman. "Rhino and I were touring with Iron Butterfly through Europe in early '71 and we knew that this band would be officially over after the summer US tour of that year, so we decided to do something together ... Bobby Caldwell (drummer) was playing the same places as we did in Europe with Johnny Winter. I personally financed the whole thing and we all wanted to go that jazz-rock direction. We got together in July '71 and played two or three weeks, then we started to look around for a lead singer and through our old manager we found out that Rod Evans wasn't working, so we contacted him and he came down to an audition and liked the situation. We jammed more and we had a recorder in the house ... so that's how the band got together." Evans cut two albums with Captain Beyond, but left the band (and the music business) in late'73 to become a medical assistant! "I was with Captain Beyond about four years and then I left – I wanted to get back into the so-called straight world somehow. You get tired of the road for whatever reason and so I went back to school and studied medicine, got my degree and worked in a hospital for five years. I was the director of respiratory therapy – a specialist field."

Even though there wasn't a great deal in the way of friendly communication between the different bands, the regular presence of Rainbow, Whitesnake and Gillan, along with the back catalogue releases, continued the popularity of Deep Purple's name in the public's eye and, for the fans at least, there was definitely a family feeling surrounding the whole thing. If there was a Purple family of sorts then Rod Evans next move showed him to be the family's bastard child. In 1980, Evans was approached by a management company with a proposition to reform Deep Purple. The same company had just been taken to court by John Kay, the owner of the name 'Steppenwolf,' for running a bogus 'Steppenwolf' with no original members. This hoax band had included guitarist Tony Flynn and keyboard player Geoff Emery. Evans was teamed up with them along with a drummer and bassist for his new version of Deep Purple. They also approached Nick Simper, who declined the invitation to get involved. Evans was drawn in hook, line and sinker when he agreed to be the only shareholder, and therefore sole risk-taker of the venture. Evans's naïve approach to the whole situation was born out when he was questioned whether or not the other Deep Purple members had been contacted: "Whether Ritchie gives his blessing or not is of no real consequence to me, as my blessing to him forming Rainbow would be of no consequence to Ritchie. I mean, if he doesn't like it I'm sorry, but we're trying." After a few gigs in Mexico in May, the name of the band was sufficient for promoters to book them at larger venues in the States, including the Swing Auditorium in San Bernadino. By August, 'Deep Purple' was booked for a gig at the 12,000-seat capacity Long Beach Arena in Los Angeles. By this time news had got to the real Deep Purple's management team that Evans was single-handedly trying to masquerade as Deep Purple. The set the bogus group performed even included numbers from the MKII and III line-ups and Evans would introduce songs with comments such as, "this is one from our 'Burn' album."

HEC Enterprises filed for an injunction at the Los Angeles Federal District Court seeking to prevent the band from using the name 'Deep Purple.' Before the court decision was taken, the management took action by placing adverts in the papers alongside those for the gig, listing the names of all the Purple members still connected with the organisation and a declaration that Blackmore, Coverdale, Gillan, Glover, Hughes, Lord and Paice would not be performing at the Long Beach Arena. Eventually the court decision decreed that Rod Evans as the sole shareholder of the 'organisation' had to pay $672,000 for damages caused by using the 'Deep Purple' name without permission.

Years after the dust had settled, Ian Paice explained, "We didn't make that money, it went all to the lawyers involved. The only chance to stop that band was to sue Rod, as he was the only one receiving money, all others were on wages. Rod got involved with some very bad people!" According to Jon Lord, "It was not just Rod who was sued – it was the organisation that was behind the fake Deep Purple who were most responsible and it was they who were hit with the greatest part of that 'very large sum of money.' Suing them was the last option there was to try to stop them. I did not enjoy having to appear in court against a guy I'd once worked with." The debacle was without doubt one of the ugliest incidents within the complex story of Deep Purple, and one that Rod Evans will probably rue forevermore.

In 1981, Swedish journalist Micke Eriksson interviewed Jon Lord and asked him if there was pressure from management and accountants to continue with Purple after they had knocked it on the head with Tommy Bolin: "Yes, actually they did. We said, 'look, we have given this everything that we can, we have given you eight years of sweat and hard work,' and that was it. But we never said 'never again,' we just put it to the side. Let Deep Purple rest for a while." Although at the time, Lord's comments may have appeared somewhat flippant, with the resurgence in heavy rock and a new generation of fans who never had the opportunity to see the band first time around, the classic MKII line-up announced to the world in April 1984 that it had reformed.

In typical 'politician' style, Jon Lord reneged on comments made on many occasions in the past by saying: "To all intents and purposes I think by the time Ritchie decided to leave, the band was over. However, forces within the band, notably David and Glenn, felt that the band should carry on and it had life left in it. I totally disagreed. To me the band was damaged almost irrevocably by Ian Gillan and Roger leaving; although David and Glenn did a marvellous job, I still felt the band wasn't the same and to replace Ritchie seemed madness."

Deep Purple has remained an entity ever since, but just like the first eight years of its career there have been plenty of line-up changes. Ian Gillan was sacked and then returned, and has remained in the band ever since. Whether or not Jon Lord stands by his earlier comment that "to replace Ritchie seemed madness" is unclear, but Blackmore quit again in 1993, and Lord finally retired from the band in 2002. Others have also come and gone, and Ian Paice is now the only original member. In the eight years that Purple existed first time around it went though four line-up changes. Since the reunion, the band has changed line-ups on no fewer than six occasions, and to some Deep Purple has become the 'Soap Opera' of rock; but we will leave the story of this part of the band's career for another day. Suffice it to say that in 1967, when Chris Curtis originally presented to Tony Edwards his vision of a musical roundabout with different musicians coming and going, it proved not to be such a barmy idea after all.

ABOUT CODA BOOKS

Most Coda books are edited and endorsed by Emmy Award winning filmmaker and concert promoter Bob Carruthers. Over the last 20 years Bob has filmed and promoted tours, concerts and made documentaries all over Britain and Europe in venues ranging from Hammersmith Odeon to Murrayfield Stadium, with artists such as Bryan Adams, Spandau Ballet, Jethro Tull, Status Quo and Katherine Jenkins.

The 'Uncensored On the Record' series explores the careers of many of music's greatest legends, encompassing a wide range of genres including classic rock, pop, heavy metal, punk, country, classical and soul.

For more information visit **www.codabooks.com**.

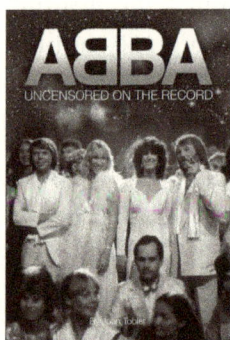

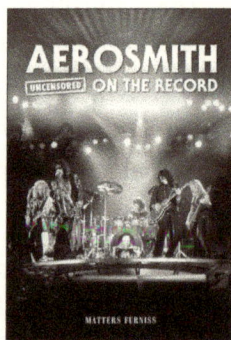

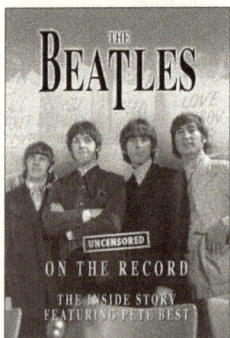

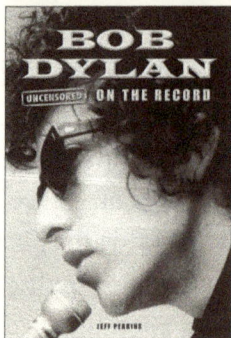

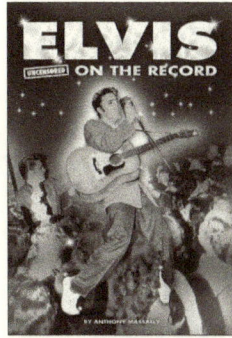
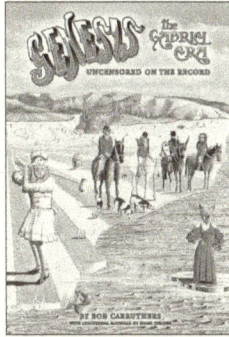

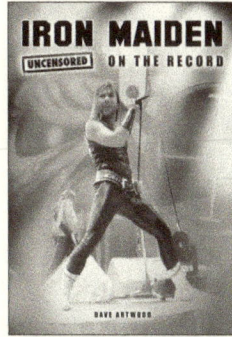
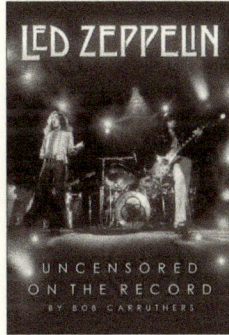

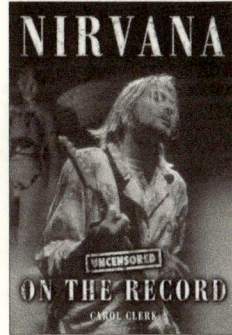

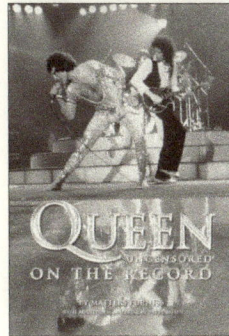
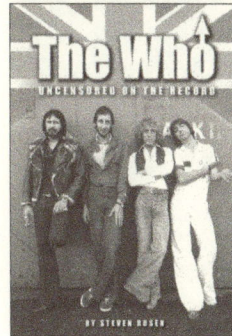

www.ingramcontent.com/pod-product-compliance
Lightning Source LLC
Chambersburg PA
CBHW021141090426
42740CB00008B/880